Reflections on 1984

Harjinder Singh

Copyright © Harjinder Singh 2014

All rights reserved.

No part of this publication may be reproduced, stored in an information storage and retrieval system, or transmitted in any form or by any means, electronic, mechanical, photocopying, recording or otherwise without written permission of Akaal Publishers.

First Published by Akaal Publishers in 2014

British Library Cataloguing in Publication Data
A catalogue record for this book is available from the British Library

ISBN 978-0-9554587-3-6

Cover Design by, Harjinder Singh of Infamous Arts

Akaal Publishers is a not for profit publisher which publishes books with timeless messages, based upon Sikh history, ethics and philosophy.

For further information see our website:
www.akaalpublishers.com

The One God is Realised With the Grace of the True Guru

Dedicated to all victims of Terrorism

CONTENTS

Preface	7 - 9
Prologue	10 - 11
30 years on ...	12 - 13
The Sikhs	14 - 22
Peaceful Campaigns	23 - 43
Bhindranwale	44 - 63
1984	64 - 97
The Homeland	98 - 102
The Civil War	103 - 116
The Post War Period	117 - 136
Relevance of Khalistan	137 - 141
Conclusion	142 - 161
My Reflections	162 - 163
Acknowledgements	164
Appendices	165 - 215
Selected Bibliography	216 - 220

Preface

This book has been written to make an objective and academic assessment of the last 30 years in relation to the events of the year 1984. For many Sikhs 1984 represents the year of the most recent holocaust that Sikhs have had to endure. It is commonly referred to as the 'Ghallughara' which translates to Holocaust.

The Sikhs are a prosperous and modern people. The Sikh Faith has become the fifth largest religion of the world, even though it only started to take form when Guru Nanak (1469 – 1539) started preaching tours in approximately 1499. It is one of the youngest world faiths and has a very modern ideology.

Most of the Sikh population resides in Punjab in India. In 1984 the Indian Government attacked the Sikh's holiest shrine in Amritsar, the Harmander Sahib, which is commonly referred to as the Golden Temple. This led to many deaths and was conducted under the pre-text of flushing out 'alleged' terrorists. Subsequently, Indira Gandhi the Prime Minister of India was assassinated and Sikhs were then publicly massacred across India in organised and co-ordinated mob violence or pogroms.

After 30 years – these events still have grave significance for Sikhs and the Indian Government. I have been compelled to write this book as most books on this recent history usually fall in to two categories, a partisan Indian Government view or a partisan Sikh view. Passions run high and the end result is usually a one-sided view. I have attempted to present both views and then draw my own conclusions from the facts I have uncovered.

The aims in writing this book were to dispel myths about the attack on Harmander Sahib and clarify the life and times of Sant Jarnail Singh Bhindranwale who is central to the attack. He is portrayed as the leader causing unrest in Punjab and the reason for attacking Harmander Sahib. Additionally, I wanted to reconstruct this recent history in terms of international law, self-determination and freedom of a people – namely the Sikhs.

I have made critical assessments of the last 20 years and the current position of Punjab does not make easy reading. Punjab has severe socio-economic problems that need to be addressed and yet the multitude of Sikh organisations both in India and outside it, seem by and large, oblivious to the rampant threats to Punjab's future sustainability and advancements.

I hope this book can achieve its aim of creating intellectual debate about the issues it attempts to cover. More importantly I hope it leads to Sikhs and non-Sikhs alike to view this recent history more objectively. I would hope that Punjabis and Sikhs that read this book start to take positive actions on both individual and community levels, to contribute to addressing Punjab's current socio-economic crisis.

Acknowledgements are made at the end of the book to thank the numerous volunteers who assisted in its compilation. Here I need to make a mention of the front cover design – it depicts a Sikh male bathing in the Sarovar (water tank) at Harmander Sahib in Amritsar. In front of him in the water is a reflection of the destroyed Akaal Takhat (Sikh Parliament) which also has blood stains. In 1984 the Indian army reduced the Akaal Takhat to rubble, destroying it through bombardment – this is what the Akaal Takhat looked like after the attack. It has become an iconic picture depicting this chapter of Sikh History, hence why I felt it was pertinent to include on the front cover. Thanks go to Harjinder Singh of Infamous Arts for the cover artwork and Aman Singh for adding the finishing touches to the design.

I hope you enjoy the book. I welcome feedback and healthy criticism. The book has been written to a very tight schedule so I apologise for any shortcomings in writing it and will endeavour to update any future editions.

Harjinder Singh
(Walsall, United Kingdom)

Prologue

In 1934, Udham Singh came to England with the single aim of avenging the Jalianwala Bagh massacre. On 13th April 1919 about 20,000 Indians had gathered at an anti-British public rally, in a park called Jalianwala Bagh in the city of Amritsar. The British forces under the command of General Reginald Dyer (1864 – 1927) opened fire on those gathered, killing hundreds. Estimates of the death toll range from 379 to 1500. Udham Singh was present at Jalianwala Bagh and witnessed the massacre. He became a revolutionary, who fought against the British colonial rule and arrived in England in 1934.

On 13th March 1940 at Caxton Hall, almost 21 years later, Udham Singh assasinated Michael O'Dwyer (1864 – 1940) shooting him in London and avenged the massacre. Michael O'Dwyer was the Lieutenant Governor of Punjab at the time of the massacre and had sanctioned the indiscriminate firing. In February 2013, David Cameron the current British Prime Minister visited Jalianwala Bagh and expressed deep regret of the massacre.

In June 1984, the Sikh Vatican - Harmander Sahib (popularly known as the Golden Temple) in Amritsar, which is 300 yards away from Jalianwala Bagh, was attacked by the Indian army in an assault named Operation Blue Star. The pretext given for the attack was that 'alleged terrorists' had taken haven at the shrine. In 2014, newly disclosed documents proved that the British Government had advised India on how to conduct the assault. Many Sikhs have not been satisfied with the government response to the disclosure, as documents have gone missing and a true picture of British involvement has not been determined. A debate in the House of Lords on 3rd March 2014 supported the proposal for an independent

UN inquiry into the massacre of Sikhs in this Indian Army Operation.[1] Thousands of innocent pilgrims lost their lives in Operation Blue Star.

In 2012, Lieutenant General Brar, one of the Army Generals leading Operation Blue Star, visited London and was attacked by four Sikhs. He survived the attack. One of his attackers lost his father and brother in Operation Blue Star, thus the attack represented a watershed for Sikhs in Britain. In 1934 Udham Singh had come to avenge Jalianwala Bagh in London, similarly in 2012 these four Sikhs had planned to avenge a massacre in the city of Amritsar.

This book explores these events and analyses the pursuit of truth, justice and liberty for Sikhs in India and the diaspora.

---

[1] The full debate can be viewed at this link
http://www.theyworkforyou.com/lords/?id=2014-03-03a.1197.0&s=warsi

30 years on ...

It's 2014 - thirty years have passed since 1984. Whilst I sit here in the UK, I reminisce about my childhood and think about what I witnessed here and in India.

The events of 1984 are synonymous in the Sikh, Indian and Khalistani psyches – it is seen as a year of immense historical significance. Many were sent to their graves and pyres.

But – why did this all occur? Who were the guilty? Who were the innocent? Who was playing political games with people's lives? Was this year 1984, the start of a war? Who was the enemy? Was it a foreign one?

Indira Gandhi. Bhindranvale. Separatists. Law & Order. President's Rule. Khalistan. Pakistan. These were all favourable terms that year. Not forgetting the others. Operation Blue Star. Assassination. Riots. Pogroms. War. Genocide. Amritdhari. Orange. Army. Militants. Terrorists.

So does this all still matter - 30 years on? It matters, as sadly, the significance of the year 1984 has increased with the passage of time for Sikhs, Hindus and Indians as a whole. Redress and justice have not been served. The significance of the events of 1984 are especially apt for the victims and perpetrators of crimes spanning from 1984 onwards.

Interestingly, the truth is more accessible and visible today than it was 30 years ago, but some still choose to ignore the facts. We have now arrived at the last stage of genocide – denial. We are witnessing victims being told to move on and forget. This is the worst possible outcome, *'it is among the surest indicators of further genocidal massacres.* [2],

The state of Punjab has moved on. Sikhs have moved on. But, people cannot simply forget. The blood in their veins does not stand still and nor does the walk towards justice; regardless of how treacherous it may be. Punjab has become a cesspit of economic and social issues. The issues leading to the war that was fought in Punjab for secession (after 1984) have not been addressed, but rather have been exacerbated.

The tormenting cloud of 1984 still looms large and will do so until there is redress. It will linger in the political systems until a true and honest assessment is made of what occurred and more pertinently what didn't occur and what hasn't occurred.

The aim is simple. Let the voice of reason resonate. I hope it does so in the preceding chapters.

---

[2] The 8 Stages of Genocide, Stanton, G.H.
http://www.genocidewatch.org/aboutgenocide/8stagesofgenocide.html

The Sikhs

The Sikh Guru's (prophets or enlightening teachers), were all revolutionary in nature and they challenged religious bigotry as well as tyrannical political rule. They were truly modern and challenged the status quo at a theological and political level. They eulogised a national pride for Sikhs and a distinct identity.

The First Sikh Guru was Guru Nanak (1469 – 1539) and his mission began in approximately 1499. He taught simplicity of faith and travelled the globe spreading his message of true devotion to God, which had no discrimination. He purposely visited religious centres and addressed religious bigotry and dogma, visiting Mecca and the Vatican in Rome.

He was succeeded by another Nine Guru's who would continue the growth of the teachings of the faith and expand its revolutionary ideals and practices. This culminated in the creation of the 'Khalsa' or 'the pure' in 1699, where the Tenth Sikh Guru completed the mission, with a distinct identity and nationhood. Sikhs would now wear articles of faith which would make them racially distinct (unshorn hair, a comb, an iron bangle, breeches and a ceremonial sword). To read more about the revolutionary faith, please see the first chapter of 'Game of Love.'[3]

The epicentre of the Sikh Faith is Harmander Sahib. Harmander Sahib is the most revered Gurdwara[4] for Sikhs, it represents heaven on earth for them. Although, Harmander Sahib commonly known as the Golden Temple

---
[3] Harjinder Singh (2008) now in its 3rd Edition (2014)
[4] Sikh place of worship, in which free food is served to all of mankind

in Amritsar[5] has a much wider significance for the whole of humanity, as people of all faiths, castes, creeds and nationalities come and bask in its spiritual environs. I would argue that it is the epicentre of all faiths; representing equality and progressiveness. It is a universal temple of God. The Sikhs as a community do themselves an unjust service, when viewing it in a restrictive singular community view. Thus, people from all walks of life, come to Amritsar; to pray and participate in community service (Seva). They attain tranquillity and many have cured their ailments by visiting and bathing in the Sarovar (the water tank which has healing powers).[6]

The Harmander Sahib has four doorways, expressing its openness to mankind; anyone can come and pray there. The Guru Granth Sahib the eternal Sikh Guru (an anthology of prayers) was first enthroned here and has always been the central point of reverence at this Gurdwara. The Guru Granth Sahib is also a universal Granth[7] which has writings from Sikhs, Muslims and Hindus. Monotheism is the faith promoted and a tolerance that anyone, of any faith, can attain God. Sant Jarnail Singh Bhindranwale (1947 – 1984) talked of these Sikh principles in the following manner when addressing some Hindus, he said, *"Who was Jaidev? Wasn't he a Hindu from amongst you? He was a Brahmin. Jaidev is sitting here in Guru Granth Sahib. If a son of a Sikh has made obeisance here he has done so at the feet of Jaidev, the Brahmin."*[8] Here, Bhindranwale gave evidence of the unity

---

[5] Amritsar is now seen as the name of the city, but it originates from Harmander Sahib as it translates to water tank of immortality (Amrit = immortality, Sar = water tank), this water tank envelopes Harmander Sahib.
[6] One such story is that of Vasu Bhardwaj
http://www.sikhiwiki.org/index.php/Vasu Bhardwaj The Indian press and Punjab daily newspapers have regular stories every few months of people being cured of their ailments after visiting the Harmander Sahib complex
[7] Anthology
[8] Sant Jarnail Singh Bhindanwale, Speech in early 1982 in Karnal.

of the Sikhs and Hindus and their respective faiths, and tolerance of one another.

Interestingly opposite Harmander Sahib is the Akaal Takhat. It is the Sikh Parliament or supreme temporal power for the Sikh Nation. The Akaal Takhat proclaims a history of defiance, it was founded to fight tyranny. The sixth Guru – Guru Hargobind founded the Akaal Takhat in 1606 AD to commence a martial tradition, so that spirituality could become entwined with the temporal. He promoted and practiced the life of a Saint and a Soldier. Taking to arms in defence of righteousness, became an integral part of the faith, culture and history of the Sikhs, herein. Now, Sikhs would draw arms when all peaceful means for solutions, had been exhausted.

The Akaal Takhat was fortified from its onset and the Guru ordered His Sikhs to bring offerings of horses and arms. The tenth and final living Guru, Guru Gobind Singh ordained that weapons were his prophet and were to be worshipped on a par to the Guru Himself, he states this in Shastar Naam Mala – a poetic description of weapons. In these weapons he includes the Tupak or a gun. Explosives with cannon balls were used by the Guru's in battle, also. Weapons were and are revered; as God's power of righteousness is invested in weapons; when used in a principled and disciplined manner. Even today, the weapons of past Sikh warriors are reverently placed on a throne at Akaal Takhat and a daily display of them takes place in the evening after the evening prayer (Rehras Sahib).

The Akaal Takhat and the Akaal Sena (God's army) - the Sikhs, would protect and uphold the integrity of faith promulgated by Harmander Sahib and all it stood for. The Sikhs would become renowned for their bravery as warriors, who protect the integrity and faith of one and all. They would fight oppression and tyranny, relinquishing risk to life; they would make daring attacks on foes, defending their strong principles of righteousness.

The Ninth Guru – Guru Tegh Bahadur (the son of Guru Hargobind) would be martyred for upholding the Hindu faith and peacefully attained martyrdom. He had taken up the cause of freedom of expression and faith, by spearheading their campaign (the Hindu's) to be able to practise their faith and stop forceful conversion by decrees of the state. In the eighteenth century the Sikhs would defend and rescue the daughters of Hindus from Afghan invaders. The Sikhs made significant sacrifices in world wars and in the free India movement. These are but a few highlights of this valiant history.

At their darkest hours, Sikhs would converge at the Akaal Takhat to discuss their key community concerns and issue edicts to be followed by the Sikh masses. The Akaal Takhat and Harmander Sahib would become targeted by those opposed to the values of universality and the revolutionary righteousness, espoused by the Sikh faith, and it's faithful. In attempts to cause maximum injury to the Sikh psyche and in vain attempts to make Sikhs extinct, invaders and rulers of the Indian sub-continent would purposely attack the Amritsar complex.

Sikh Nationalism

Today, we have many nations in the world order and it is accepted by the United Nations that people of a particular nation have a right to self-determination. The French revolution and the overthrow of many monarchical rulers led to the modern nation state, in which sovereignty is held by a 'people' through a mutually agreed political process. Most of these modern states determine their power politics through democratic elections, the underlying principles being that no-one is deemed to be a ruler by birth or ancestry, all citizens are equals, and popular support will determine the future of the nation.

Nations and nationality are defined by unifying factors. The simple ones are a national anthem, a cultural infinity and adherence to the norms and values of that particular nation. Although, some 'people' may view themselves as a distinct nation, they may not necessarily have a geographical sovereign rule or state. This is where the case of the Sikh nationalism enters the debate.

In 200 years (1499 – 1699) the Sikh Guru's had set the foundations for radical political change as cultural and ideological transformations had been instilled in the populace that became their Sikhs (disciples). The Guru's had bravely challenged caste prejudice, gender inequality and had promoted a social ethos of a community that served mankind – serving free food wherever they went. All Social Reform programmes have their opponents, this was no different for Sikhs, the invading Muslims and hereditary Hindu Kings, saw this as a front to their seats of power, as indeed it was. This led to Sikhs fighting injustice and tyranny from the onset of their faith to the present day.

Giuseppe Mazzini (1805 – 1872) was a key figure in the unification of Italy and a theorist of the modern state. He stated that the four key traits of a nation were a common language, territory, literature and ethnicity.[9] The Sikhs had their own language Gurmukhi. Sikh literature (scriptures) were penned in Gurmukhi. The Gurmukhi script was created by the second Sikh Guru, Guru Angad

---

[9] Stefano Recchia & Nadia Urbinati (2009) in the introduction of "A Cosmopolitanism of Nations." Giuseppe Mazzini

and today it is used to write Indian Punjabi. The majority Sikh population has always come from the Punjab – this is where territorial loyalty lies for the Sikhs and the Sikhs are a distinct ethnic group. Thus, the Sikhs have the traits of a nation as theorised by Mazzini.

Two previous Sikh Sovereign states have been in existence. The first was that of Banda Singh Bahadur (1670 – 1716 AD) who invaded Punjab and conquered parts of it to set up a Sovereign Sikh state from 1710 to 1716 AD. The second was led by Maharajah (King) Ranjit Singh (1780 – 1839 AD). He successfully united the Sardars (Sikh Chieftains) into one state from 1801 to 1839 AD without interruption. It fell into disarray after the death of Ranjit Singh and was finally annexed by the British in 1847 after two very bloody Anglo-Sikh wars. These two periods of sovereignty are seen as glorious and are idealistically sought by protagonists of Khalistan (a separate Sikh State). A nation that has ruled once remembers this past, especially when their community feels oppressed and discriminated against, by their present government.

The opportunity to carve out a separate Sikh homeland at Indian independence (1947 AD) was surpassed by the Sikhs and instead they chose to align themselves with the Congress Party and join India (as opposed to joining Pakistan). This led to a major displacement of the Sikh population and a loss of half their historical Gurdwaras.

Punjab (their homeland) was partitioned to make two Punjabi states, in both Pakistan and within India. The partition led to a mass exodus on both sides of the border and it is estimated that 1 million people lost their lives in the communal violence that ensued, the majority of losses occurred in Punjab. The Sikhs had high hopes, thinking that they would enjoy the glow of freedom in the new India, these hopes were destroyed when the legal frameworks for governance of India started to emerge.

Self-Determination

"Self-determination denotes the legal right of people to decide their own destiny in the international order. Self-determination is a core principle of international law, arising from customary international law, but also recognized as a general principle of law, and enshrined in a number of international treaties. For instance, self-determination is protected in the United Nations Charter and the International Covenant on Civil and Political Rights as a right of "all peoples."[10]

There are two types of self-determination, internal and external. Internal self-determination is about determining policy and enactments of law within a state by its people. This could be by section of the population or the whole population, through campaigns on specific issues or referendums. *"Internal self-determination can also mean that right to exercise cultural, linguistic, religious or (territorial) political autonomy within the boundaries of the existing state."*[11] From the inception of the Indian constitution Sikhs had campaigned for this internal self-determination within the union of India as Article 25 stated that Sikhs were essentially Hindus and not a distinct faith. Sikhs have never signed the Indian constitution.

India in 'theory' is a secular state it has a 1.27 billion population. The Religious demographics of India are 80%

---

[10] http://www.law.cornell.edu/wex/self_determination_international_law
[11] http://www.academia.edu/2967647/RIGHT_OF_PEOPLES_TO_SELF-DETERMINATION_IN_THE_PRESENT_INTERNATIONAL_LAW

Hindu, 12% Muslim, 2.5% Christian and 2% Sikh. The Hindu majority obviously have the most influence and are essentially the electorate for any incumbent national government. The political parties in India thus do have to concede to demands of the Hindu majority and in some cases the political parties will electioneer to Hindu sentiments. In essence this is what the Congress Party did with the Sikhs in the 1980's – it played communal politics with the lives of Sikhs. This will be explored throughout the preceding chapters.

External self-determination is wanting secession or setting up sovereignty in a new state for a 'people', in effect becoming independent from an existing state. Scotland's historical vote for independence this autumn could lead to external self-determination. The Sikhs in India had sought external determination after 1986 – this will also be explored in the coming chapters.

Peaceful Campaigns

Let me say, with the risk of appearing ridiculous, that the true revolutionary is guided by strong feelings of love. It is impossible to think of an authentic revolutionary without this quality.

Che Guevera
(1968:389)

Sikhs are peace loving and believe in equality of the human race. There is no racial, gender, class or caste superiority – everyone has an equal footing. Sikhs pray daily for the well-being of mankind and end their daily supplication prayer with "Tere Bhane Sarbat Da Bhalla" which translates to – may everyone prosper. Here no distinction is made, Sarbat means everyone. This universal love permeates Sikh theology, Sikh lifestyle, Sikh history and is exemplified by Sikhs when they fight injustice not just for themselves, but for the whole of mankind.

Indian Independence

At the time of India's Independence, Sikhs aligned themselves with the Indian Congress Party and joined the newly formulated India in 1947. Promises by both Jawarhar Lal Nehru and Mahatma Gandhi[12] assured the Sikhs, that they would enjoy the glow of freedom in this new nation state.[13] However, Nehru's clear dislike of the Sikhs is evident in his autobiography where he speaks of his dislike for the top-knot and beard which are kept unshorn by Sikhs, *"I do not fancy beards or moustaches or topknots, but I have no desire to impose my canons of taste*

---

[12] The two leading figures of the Indian National Congress which led the India Free Movement. Gandhi is known for his peaceful agitations whereas Nehru was the political leader of the Congress and India's first Prime Minister. It would be Nehru's family who would eventually become a dynasty in the Indian political make-up, his daughter Indira Gandhi would be a future Prime Minister.

[13] Jaijee (1999: 3-4), *Politics of Genocide*, Ajanta Publications, Delhi

on others, though I must confess, in regard to beards, that I inwardly rejoiced when Amanullah began to deal with them in summary fashion in Kabul."[14] Amanullah Khan was a King of Afghanistan who outlawed keeping one's beard. This dislike of Nehru's of those keeping unshorn hair bore witness to the policies that would be implemented in the free India, with regards to the Sikhs. *"A policy letter dated October 10, 1947 from the Punjab Government informed the Deputy Commissioners that 'the Sikhs, as a community, were a lawless people and were thus a menace to the law-abiding Hindus in the province', and called upon the Deputy Commissioners to take special measures against them."*[15] The Deputy Commissioners are executive heads of administrative districts of the state; they have considerable powers over these districts. These orders clearly go against the espoused 'secular' nature of India.

This racism was a shock to the Sikhs who had loyally made sacrifices for the independence movement, *"During the freedom struggle, 73 of 121 persons executed were the Sikhs and 2147 of 2664 sentenced to life imprisonment ... were the Sikhs. In the Jalianwala Bagh massacre ... out of 1302 ... gunned down by General Dyer, 799 were the Sikhs."*[16] The Sikhs made disproportionate sacrifices for the freedom movement, freeing India and Pakistan from colonialism. Unfortunately, these efforts were not justly rewarded when independence did dawn. Majority population politics came to the fore, and the Sikhs as a minority became just a small voice amongst the popular voices of the Hindu and Muslim populations.

---

[14] Nehru J (1980: 471), *Jawarlal Nehru An Autobiography*, Oxford University Press, New Delhi. Amanullah Khan was the ruler of Afghanistan for a short period of time, he outlawed beards.
[15] Kapur Singh (1979: 209-210), *Saachi Saakhi*, Navyug Publishers, Chandni Chowk, Delhi
[16] Sangat Singh (1995:202) *The Sikhs in History*, New York

The dawn of Indian Independence meant that 40% of the Sikh population had to be re-housed from what now became Pakistan and this resulted in a loss of all Gurdwaras in Pakistan (half of the significant historical shrines of the Sikh faith). In this new India, Sikhs had to now register their weddings under the Hindu Marriage Act in order to be seen as lawful husband and wife.[17] The Sikhs refused to sign the Indian Constitution in 1950 as it defined Sikhs as Hindus[18] and not a distinct faith or racial group.[19]

All of the states of India were linguistically defined, thus the state's native language would become its primary language (as opposed to Hindi which was the national language). India is a very diverse nation and making concessions for states in this way would ensure a state and national identity.

In Punjab this linguistic preference didn't prevail and instead Hindi was made the state language as opposed to Punjabi. As stated previously the Punjabi language's script was created by the second Sikh Guru and is called

---

[17] The Sikh Marriage Act has now been ratified by the Indian Parliament in June 2012
[18] Article 25 of the Indian Constitution, which states the following,
Freedom of conscience and free profession, practice and propagation of religion -
(1) Subject to public order, morality and health and to the other provisions of this Part, all persons are equally entitled to freedom of conscience and the right freely to profess, practice and propagate religion.
(2) Nothing in this article shall affect the operation of any existing law or prevent the State from making any law -
(a) regulating or restricting any economic, political or other secular activity which may be associated with religious practice;
(b) providing for social welfare and reform or the throwing open of Hindu religious institutions of a public character to all classes and sections of Hindus.
Explanation I – The wearing and carrying of kirpans shall be deemed to be included in the profession of the Sikh religion.
Explanation II – **In sub-Clause (b) of clause (2), the reference to Hindus shall be construed as including a reference to persons professing the Sikh, Jaina or Buddhist religion, and the reference to Hindu religious institutions shall be construed accordingly.**
[19] The British during the Raj recognised the Sikhs as a separate faith and in modern day Britain, Sikhs are also seen as a racial group as defined by the Race Relations Act 1976

Gurmukhi. Sikh scriptures are written in this Gurmukhi script.

The Hindu right wing pigeonholed the claim for the Punjabi language, as a separatist demand by the Sikhs, portraying it as an exemplar that Sikhs wanted their own fiefdom. This resulted in Hindus in Punjab voting for Hindi to become the state's primary language. The Sikh leaders denied this claim of separatism, but in turn did see this as a challenge to their minority status and a threat to their assimilation into the majority Hindu fold.

The Sikhs made up 2% of the population of India and were not even a majority in Punjab. So what choice did the Sikhs have, but to start peaceful campaigns to realise the freedoms they felt were assured in this new nation? Sikhs had expected to be protected as a religious minority, as they had been by the British in colonial rule and the Sikhs had chosen to join India as they felt they would achieve equal status in the new free India.

Peaceful agitations to achieve the linguistic organisation they had expected in India, commenced soon after independence in 1947. These agitations culminated in a Punjabi Suba[20] campaign which led to a truncated Punjab in 1966.[21] In this new Punjab Sikhs would become the majority community and finally the Punjabi language would get the primary language status. Now Sikhs made up approximately 60% of the state population, thus Sikhs could now meet the demands of their community with more ease.

State of Emergency (1975 – 1977)

---

[20] A state in which Punjabi would be the primary state language
[21] Leading to the creation of a new state of Haryana; loss of some areas to Himachal Pradesh; and creation of Chandigarh as union territory.

Sikhs would come to the fore in national politics once again during the tenure of Indira Gandhi as Prime Minister. In 1975 Indira Gandhi was found guilty of election fraud by an Allahabad court and was barred from contesting elections for 6 years. The ban meant she would also have to relinquish her seat as a member of parliament and her cabinet role as Prime Minister. Many expected her to appeal the ruling and win on appeal.

She instead took the drastic step of using an obscure loop hole in the Indian law to engineer the declaration of a state of emergency; citing internal disturbances as a reason to declare the emergency. So for a 21 month period from 25th June 1975 to 21st March 1977 - Indira Gandhi ruled by decree, elections and parliament were suspended, and an authoritarian rule ensued. Civil liberties were curbed and much of her political opponents were imprisoned, as they were rightly protesting at this halt in democracy for spurious reasons. The press was censored and her son Sanjay Gandhi rolled out a mass sterilisation campaign in which mostly the economically poor; usually fell victim to being forcibly sterilised[22].

Lovers of freedom and democracy and political opponents of Indira Gandhi immediately protested against the emergency and they were dealt with swiftly, by being imprisoned. This left hardly any political opposition for Indira Gandhi, even though she had also ostracised a lot of her own cabinet as well. This is when the Sikhs took up the baton and started campaigns to oppose the state of emergency.

---

[22] To gain a vivid picture of the state of emergency through fiction, one is advised to read *"A fine Balance"* by Rohinton Mistry (2006)

With no major contenders left to protest against the emergency; the Sikhs through the Akali Dal[23] launched a national campaign in Amritsar known as the "Campaign to Save Democracy". Throughout the campaign most of the Sikh leaders who avoided arrest, did so, by taking refuge in the Harimander Sahib in Amritsar. The police came out in force and arrested protesting Sikhs. Over 40,000 Sikhs were imprisoned as part of the "Save Democracy Movement.[24] *"It has been argued that Mrs Gandhi never forgave the Akalis for their opposition to the emergency."*[25]

Indira Gandhi wanted to meet with the protest leaders but Sant Harchand Singh Longowal[26] who was leading the protests flatly refused to come to the negotiation table and stated, *"The question before us is not whether Indira Gandhi should continue to be prime minister or not. The point is whether democracy in this country is to survive or not. The democratic structure stands on three pillars, namely a strong opposition, independent judiciary and free press. Emergency has destroyed all these essentials."*[27]

The iron fist of dealing with protestors against the emergency through mass arrests, censorship and intimidation, meant that very little appetite for opposition was left in the Indian masses or political opponents of Indira Gandhi. The Sikhs thus continued alone, spearheading the campaign and courting arrest on the night

---

[23] Akali Dal translates to Immortal Confederation. It is the major Sikh Political Party and is also known as the Shromani Akali Dal.
[24] Grewal (1990: 214) *The Sikhs of the Punjab*, Cambridge, Cambridge University Press; Malhotra (1989: 178), *Indira Gandhi: A Personal and Political Biography*,London/Toronto, Hodder and Stoughton
[25] Tridivesh Singh Maini in, *"The Politics of Religion in South & South East Asia"* by Ishtaq Ahmed, Taylor & Francis (2011: 72)
[26] The then President of the Akali Dal
[27] Gurmit Singh, (1991, 2:39) *A History of Sikh Struggles*, New Delhi, Atlantic Publishers and Distributors,

of no moon (Masiya) – symbolising the diminishing freedoms in India.

Sikhs were hailed as the last bastion of democracy[28] and they continued to court arrest until the end of the emergency. The Sikhs had successfully continued their historical tradition of fighting for freedom for all Indians.

Amnesty International estimated that 140,000 people had been arrested and held without trial during the emergency period. Sikhs made up approximately 30% of those arrested in the state of emergency.

Once again the Sikhs disproportionately spearheaded a freedom movement, from their 2% population in India. Longowal would later go on to argue that, first the Sikhs fought for the freedom of India from the British. Secondly, the Sikhs led the freedom movement from the state of emergency and today, the Sikhs are fighting for the demands of the Dharam Yudh Morcha.[29]

Indian politics being the amazing hotpot of diversity that it is, meant that Indira Gandhi lost the election in 1977. She was re-elected again on 14 January 1980, as the coalition government couldn't hold office through a majority. She dismissed all state governments and ordered fresh elections which meant the Akali's lost to the Congress Party in Punjab.

Anandpur Sahib Resolution

Punjab had experienced the green revolution and had yielded gains in farming, but the youth of Punjab were disenfranchised and were experiencing unprecedented

---

[28] Kumar & Sieberer, (1990: 250) *The Sikh Struggle: Origin, Evolution and Present Phase*, Delhi, Chanakya Publishers
[29] The Dharam Yudh Morcha was launched in August 1982 to achieve more rights of Punjabi's in India, it was spearheaded by the Akali Dal under Longowal's leadership

levels of unemployment. It was at this point that the Akali's brought the Anandpur Sahib Resolution to the table. It was a set of demands to start a campaign against the state and central governments of the Congress Party. The resolution was originally drafted in 1975 and had subsequent revisions, but the major points were consistent throughout. I will briefly outline some of the demands which were applicable to all Punjabis and make commentary on each of the resolutions.

Resolution 1
- Decentralisation of power to states due to emergency in 1975; attempting to avoid dictatorial rule in the future by setting up a real federal system, whereby, such authoritarian rule cannot impede on the freedoms of Indians again. *"As such, the Shiromani Akali Dal emphatically urges upon the Janata Government to take cognizance of the different linguistic and cultural sections, religious minorities as also the voice of millions of people and recast the constitutional structure of the country on real and meaningful federal principles to obviate the possibility of any danger to the unity and integrity of the country and, further, to enable the states to play a useful role for the progress and prosperity of the Indian people in their respective areas by a meaningful exercise of their powers."*

This resolution is a clear example of internal self-determination in which the Sikh political party had articulated more autonomy in a true federal system. In modern terms it can be viewed as a resolution for devolution, much like that of Wales and Scotland in the United Kingdom or that of state powers in the United States of America (USA).

Its implementation would have ensured more state autonomy for all Indian states and avoidance of abuses of power from the central government, which had occurred in the state of emergency. This resolution would have empowered the Indian populace.

Resolution 2
- Chandigarh, which was originally supposed to be the capital of Punjab, to be handed back to the Punjab.[30]

- Merging Punjabi speaking areas from other states back into Punjab, this is in reference to areas that were lost when Punjab was truncated in 1966.

- *"The arbitrary and unjust Award given by Mrs. Indira Gandhi during the Emergency on the distributions of Ravi-Beas waters should be revised on the universally accepted norms and principles, and justice be done to Punjab."*

This is about the fair usage of Punjab's primary natural resource of river water, as the river water is diverted to irrigate lands in other states and produces electricity for them. This is a case of discrimination against the Punjab, as the state receives no recompense for the depletion of this natural resource.

Punjab's main industry is agriculture and Punjabi farmers experience great difficulty and expense in watering their fields, when in actual fact they shouldn't in this water rich state. The diversion of river waters of the state creates economic burden and disparity for electricity. Punjab has

---

[30] This would have meant more economic vibrancy of Punjab due to the economical influence of the city. The city became union territory when Punjab was truncated in 1966 and it became the joint capital of the Punjabi and Haryana states.

regular power cuts as electricity is required to irrigate fields as it is required to pump surface water to irrigate agriculture.

- A reservation quota for Sikhs in the army, protecting them as a martial race and minority; as had been the case during the British Raj.

Resolution 3

- Breaking control of monopolistic capitalist hold on the economy and redistributing wealth.

- Eradicating unemployment and starting an unemployment benefit.

- Fair taxation – to be fairer to the poor and taxing the wealthy more.
- Fair reservation for scheduled castes and supporting them financially.

All the above economic proposals would have lead to more economic parity for all Punjabis. For obvious reasons these would have not been appealing to wealthy capitalists, but the appeal of these proposals would have been wide-reaching for the majority of Punjabi's who had small holdings of land or the poor.

Resolution 4

- Second language status for Punjabi in neighbouring states of Punjab – where Punjabi is the second language in terms of population but other languages are given this status.

Second language status was granted to the Telugu language in Haryana based on 0.02 of the population speaking it.[31] This was purposely done to devalue the linguistic value of Punjabi for Sikhs living in Haryana.

Resolution 9

- Broadcast of Darbar Sahib Kirtan[32] on Radio at all times, internationally. Sikhs will pay for it, but the government can control it.

This demand was about broadcasting Sikh prayers which are peaceful and uplifting. Sikhs would bore the costs of relay, yet even implementing this resolution took years.

Dharam Yudh Morcha

The above demands were articulated in a campaign of peaceful civil disobedience agitations[33] called the Dharam Yudh Morcha. These agitations included road blocks, strikes from work, stopping canal waters and

---

[31] *"Old-timers say the Tamil was declared as the second language just to give a rebuff to Punjab. Since it was the Punjabi suba agitation that had led to formation of Haryana, Bansi Lal thought, 'Let any language other than Punjabi be the second language of the state'. Hence, Tamil became the second language even though there might not have be even a single Tamil native family in the state at that point of time', said a former bureaucrat."* Bansi Lal was the Chief Minister of Haryana, as reported in DNA India by Ajay Bharadwaj, Sunday 7th March, 2010

[32] Hymn singing from Harmander Sahib/Golden Temple in Amritsar

[33] This campaign was called the Dharam Yudh Morch – translated it means, war of righteousness.

courting arrest. The campaign was led by the moderate Akali's and supported by Sant Jarnail Singh Bhindranwale. They gained mass support for the campaign, which was for the benefit of all Punjabis, Hindus, Muslims, Christians and Sikhs. The majority of the demands were economic in nature. The demands of extra religious rights were minor aspects of the campaign but were purposely sensationalised to create political slur, communalism and a war like atmosphere.

The Anandpur Sahib Resolution was although named with reference to the name of the site of the creation of the Khalsa on purpose. Anandpur is the city where the Tenth Sikh Guru – Guru Gobind Singh founded the initiation ceremony for Sikhs in 1699. It was in effect the first Sikh State, the township had been founded by the Ninth Guru. Anandpur translates to the 'City of Bliss.' Thus there were Sikh elements to the resolution, but this Sikh dressing of the resolution was insignificant and the thrust of the document was to ensure equal rights and civil liberties for all Punjabis and not just the Sikhs. Now, we will turn our focus to the politics of these peaceful campaigns and the historical backdrop.

During the state of emergency Sikhs had been the most vocal opponents of Indira Gandhi. Specifically two leaders were her significant opponents in the campaign, namely Longowal of the Akali party and Sant Kartar Singh Bhindranwale[34]. They were the ones who led to her eventual fall as the Prime Minister.

So she had a clear agenda to pursue against the Sikhs when she regained power. She manipulated the Dharam

---

[34] The predecessor of Sant Jarnail Singh Bhindranwale, Sant Kartar Singh died after a car accident in 1977. Sant Jarnail Singh was now leading the Dharam Yudh Morcha in partnership with Longowal.

Yudh Morcha and the demands of the Sikhs at every juncture; this time, she would refuse to meet or accede to the demands of Longowal who had refused to come to the negotiating table during the emergency. To realise the demands of the Anandpur Sahib Resolution mass civil disobedience was being implemented by the Akalis' with approximately 250,000 Punjabis courting arrest between 1982 and 1984.[35]

Also the Akali's were playing opposition party politics as the Congress Party had come into power in the Punjab, but diffusion of the situation and campaign, were not at all out of sight. The Akali's were actually vying for a compromise to make a settlement and agree an accord with the government which would stop the peaceful agitations.[36]

Sant Jarnail Singh Bhindranwale had risen to prominence and was seen as the more militant voice of the Dharam Yudh Morcha whereas Longowal was seen as the moderate voice of the Sikhs. The next chapter will fully discuss the phenomenon that was Bhindranwale, but here it needs to be mentioned that his predecessor Sant Kartar Singh had already crossed paths with Indira Gandhi during the emergency.

During the Dharam Yudh Morcha (1982 – 1984) a mass media frenzy was created of lawlessness in Punjab prior to June 1984. An image of Punjab being over-run by violence and killings in acts of terrorism was constructed by the Indian State apparatus, facilitated by many commentators, journalists and servants of the state. The true threat that existed was mass support and participation

---

[35] Game of Love, Harjinder Singh (2008)
[36] This did occur but it was too late by then, in July 1985 a Rajiv Gandhi & Longowal Accord was agreed.

in the civil disobedience protests of the Sikhs, which were all peaceful.

On one hand we have this governmental view of lawlessness and on the other we have that of independently minded journalists, commentators and seekers of justice, including members of the state apparatus who bravely advocated the truth. There were crimes being committed on both sides of the divide; from the evidence available, it seems like there was a minor law and order problem, and the state purposely manipulated this, turning it into a threat to national security, when it clearly wasn't.

Fake Encounters

The state instigated violence, by targeting Sikhs who were peacefully campaigning or completely innocent people were arrested and tortured. One example of state excesses were those of fake encounters, whereby the security forces would torture to death or simply kill somebody in custody and then declare that the offender died in an exchange of fire. One case is highlighted by Bhindranwale; *"Bhai Gurmeet Singh of Dhulkot, the only son of his parents ... was caught. His nails were pulled out and salt was poured (over the wounds), his hands were burnt by placing candles under the palms of his hands. Then Bhullar sent a wireless message to the Chief Minister of Punjab, stating that his hands had been burnt, his nails had been pulled out and salt poured over them but he would not say anything except The Timeless God/Truth is eternal and God is the Wonderful Englightener. Then, the words came out of this proud man's mouth that this man should be shot to death. That is how he was martyred."*[37] Bhullar was a senior police officer.

---

[37] Sant Jarnail Singh Ji Bhindranwale, Speech in February 1983. Videos about such fake encounters can be viewed at http://www.ensaaf.org/multimedia/tag/punjab-police/

Tully and Jacob describe how the Chief Minister of Punjab, Darbara Singh, ordered fake encounters, *"He did order the police to take action against those terrorists they could not get hold of ... (via) 'encounters' – a euphemism for cold-blooded murder by the police. Darbara Singh admitted as much to me. On another occasion, when Satish Jacob and I both met him, the former Chief Minister said, 'Encounters did take place and they were killed. I told my senior police officers, 'You kill the killers and I will take the responsibility.'"* [38] And again, *"Bhinder told me that ten people he described as 'Bhindranwale's do or die men' had been shot by the police and that more than 1600 had been arrested."* [39]

There is clear evidence pointing the finger sharply back at the security forces for engaging in unlawful killings with impunity. In these fake encounters only Sikhs would die and no casualties or even injuries would be suffered by the Police. If the accusation of Sikh extremists/terrorists going on killing sprees can be seen as credible; then it follows that the state terrorism of the Indian security forces and administration can also be seen as valid.

Lawlessness in Punjab (1982-1984)

A closer study of the actual facts of lawlessness does give us a different picture. More than 150 people had died in 1983 through the 'nonviolent protest action that has sometimes ended in shooting and killing in the last eight months.'[40] Shootings by the police occurred on those peacefully protesting.

---

[38] Tully & Jacob, (1985: 106) Amritsar, Mrs Gandhi's Last Battle, Rupa, New Delhi
[39] Ibid p.108
[40] William K Stevens, New York Times, 3 May 1983
http://www.nytimes.com/1983/05/03/world/sikh-holyleader-talks-of-violence.html

Zail Singh the President of India confirmed that 23 Sikhs had been shot dead for peacefully attempting to set up a road block as part of their agitation and a further 6 had been killed for shouting slogans.[41] By 1983 more than 100,000 people had courted arrest.[42]

When investigating the killings of people in Punjab; we have to take into account the deaths of those who were peacefully protesting and were killed by the security forces. This point needs to be made as many of the cases that are mentioned in the Government White Paper of 1984, as acts of violence and alleged terrorism, are actually referring to the killings of Sikhs alone and not government officials or Hindus as has been suggested.

The Government of India White Paper on the Punjab Agitation (July 1984) is purposely ambiguous when tallying up acts of violence and calling them terrorism. This was purposely done to add to the myth of lawlessness. The killings in the 1978 clash with the Nirankaris[43] and the shooting at Mehta in 1981 when Bhindranwale was arrested are purposely added to the crime statistics of the White Paper to add to the myth of lawlessness. But when one studies these two examples, one will learn that 13 peacefully protesting Sikhs were killed by Nirankaris in 1978, and at Mehta in 1981, at least 12 Sikhs were killed by the Police who opened fire on the congregation after Bhindranwale had courted arrest. See Appendix 5 for a

---

[41] Zail Singh in "Disappearances in Punjab," A documentary by Ram Narayan Kumar and Lorenz Skerjanz, 1995.
[42] William K Stevens, New York Times, 3 May 1983
http://www.nytimes.com/1983/05/03/world/sikh-holyleader-talks-of-violence.html
[43] Thirteen Sikhs died after clashing with a sect called Nirankaris. The Sikhs argue they were peacefully protesting and were attacked by the Nirankaris. Many more Sikhs were injured in the clash. The Nirankaris suffered no casualties and the Nirankaris accused of the killings and violence would go on to be exonerated in a trial held in Haryana. This added to more ill-feelings with the Indian state and Nirankaris and the Sikhs. These deaths led to an awakening of injustice in India for many Sikhs.

description of the heavy handedness that the government wanted to employ when dealing with Bhindranwale in 1981, General Sinha describes his role and the advice he gave to the government.

As for actual militants or terrorists, 'There have never been more than about 500 of them, the authorities say.'[44] This is in reference to those Sikhs accused of taking to armed actions, assassinations and acts of terror as defined by the Indian state. So these 500 out of the 14 million Sikhs in India caused a threat to national security and stability; leading to the tumultuous events of 1984? So even by government accounts of criminality or terrorism in Sikhs, the sums amounting to a real threat did not add up.

Also, above Tully & Jacob quote that 1600 Sikhs had been arrested. This adds supporting evidence to the notion that innocent Sikhs were being falsely arrested and accused of crimes they had no involvement in. What could be seen as a minor law and order problem was made into war mongering. *"It is noteworthy that of all the cases listed in the White Paper it was only in eleven that the attackers are even alleged to be Sikh. In all the other cases the assailants were unknown."*[45] The White Paper also gives reasons for conducting Operation Blue Star and the use of the army to manage law and order in Punjab.

Even supporters of the Congress Party and those individuals that despised Bhindranwale, like Kushwant Singh, had to admit, *"The police was rarely able to identify*

---

[44] William K Stevens, New York Times, 3 April 1984
http://www.nytimes.com/1984/04/03/world/with-punjabthe-prize-sikh-militants-spread-terror.html
[45] Sandhu, (1999: xxvii) *"Struggle for Justice"* , Sikh Educational & Religious Foundation

or arrest the culprits. Its only method of dealing with the menace was to organize fake encounters..." [46]

Furthermore, *"More than 100 people have been killed since the terror reached a peak in mid-February and more than 300 since the start of the 20-month-old agitation on behalf of greater autonomy for the Sikhs' home state of Punjab that spawned the terrorist campaign."*[47] This was reported in April 1984. If we accept that 300 deaths occurred in 20 months; that works out to be 15 deaths each month. These figures would need to be compared with comparable statistics of other Indian states to ascertain the scale of the 'lawlessness' that existed in Punjab. For example Sinha et al inform us that, *"In Delhi alone in the year 1983, 244 persons were murdered* (Statesman, July 1, 1984)"[48] Nayar confirms that in Uttar Pardesh(U.P.) in 1980 there were 5,422 murders and in 1981, 5068 murders. In comparison with Punjab for the same years there were 620 killings in 1980 and 544 in 1981. Even if population differences are taken into account, it is still clear that in comparison to Punjab, U.P. had a higher rate of murders.

The alleged lawlessness in Punjab possibly warranted a case for better policing; but the use of the army is just incomprehensible. Indira Gandhi had become very accustomed to using the army during the emergency period, as part of her high-handed approach to rule. This theme of domineering oppression continued with Punjabis during her reign, from 1980 – 1984.

---

[46] Kushwant Singh: in The Punjab Story, edited by Amarjit Kaur et al, (1989:9), Roli Books,
[47] William K Stevens, New York Times, 3 April 1984
http://www.nytimes.com/1984/04/03/world/with-punjabthe-prize-sikh-militants-spread-terror.html
[48] Sinha et al, (1984: 38-39) *Army Action in Punjab: Prelude and Aftermath*, Samta Era, Delhi,

Now, moving to the crucial year of 1984; 298 people were killed in 5 months preceding Operation Blue Star.[49] The question that needs to be posed is - how many Sikhs/Punjabis were killed for peacefully protesting? Yes, 298 deaths occurred, but by whose hands remains a doubt.

Of all the books and sources I have trawled, I have not found a satisfying response from the Indian state of how the situation statistically was actually a concern for the whole nation; in terms of alleged 'terrorism'. I have searched for empirical data to support the claims of the government of a real problem with law and order, but have been unable to unearth evidence pointing to the existence of a real threat.

Yes, the peaceful civil rights movement (Dharam Yudh Morcha) was a concern for the nation in terms of the mass support from the Punjabi people, but that did not necessarily align with this alleged 'terrorism.' Bhindranwale and Longowal had both consistently condemned acts of lawlessness.

Bhindranwale was projected as a war mongering cleric by the media and government, which in the 1980's was one and the same thing. There was one state controlled TV channel and the government could sensor the media and reporting of news.

We need to now discuss the role of Bhindranwale and ask why he is now eulogised by Sikhs around the globe. He fought against the Indian Army with his militant companions from within the Harmander Sahib (Golden Temple) complex in Amritsar. This was the culmination of the peaceful civil rights movement of the Akalis.

---

[49] Hardgrave & Kochanek (2008: 175), *Indian Government and Politics in a Developing Nation*. Engage Learning

Views on Bhindranwale are usually at polar opposites, people either love him or despise him. Let us now dissect the facts through an analysis of the evidence in the next chapter.

Bhindranwale

My mission is to administer Amrit[50], to explain the meanings of Gurbani[51] and to teach Gurbani to those around me; ... that a Hindu should be a true Hindu, a Muslim should be a true Muslim, and a Sikh should be a true Sikh."

Sant Jarnail Singh Bhindranwale, 22 February 1984

Who was Bhindranwale?

Bhindranwale's full name is Sant Jarnail Singh Bhindranwale. He was appointed the 14th Leader of the Damdami Taksal[52] in 1977 – which is a religious educational institute that traces its lineage back to the times of Guru Gobind Singh (1666 AD – 1708 AD). It was at his appointment as the leader of the seminary that 'Jarnail Singh' inherited the honorific titles of 'Sant' and 'Bhindranwale' making him Sant Jarnail Singh Bhindranwale.

Sant translates to Saint and Bhindran – is the name of the village previously associated with the 11th Leader of the seminary Sant Sundar Singh, Bhindran wale – translates to being of Bhindran village. All the subsequent leaders of the seminary after Sant Sundar Singh have also been known as Bhindranwale. Bhindranwale was a simple farmer who entered the tutelage of the 12th Leader of the Taksal (Sant Gurbhachan Singh) and served under the 13th Leader of the Taksal Sant Kartar Singh. Early on, he was known as 'Abhyasee,' which translates to a person who continuously engrosses themselves in prayer.

---

[50] Initiate Sikhs, Amrit is the ambrosial nectar that is administered in the initiation ceremony of Sikhs

[51] Gurbani translates to the "Guru's word" which is the Sikh Scriptures

[52] A Sikh Seminary see www.damdamitaksal.com

Nirankari Clash

Bhindranwale rose to fame in 1978 when 13 Sikhs were slaughtered for peacefully protesting against the Nirankari cult in Amritsar on Vaisakhi[53]. He started campaigning for justice through the law courts of India to get the culprits punished who had gunned down and attacked the 13 Sikhs.[54] His close confidant Bhai Amrik Singh[55] seized the land upon which the 13 Sikhs had been killed; to construct a memorial for their fallen souls.

Bhindranwale started a campaign of preaching and teaching Punjabis[56] about the sacrilegious practices of the Nirankari cult. This is where animosity with Lala Jagat Narain began, he was a strong supporter of the Nirankaris and even defended them as a witness, in the eventual court case, against them for killing the Sikhs[57]. Narain would later get assassinated.

Preaching Tours

Bhindranwale spent his early years as the leader of the Damdami Taksal by going on preaching tours of Sikhism in villages and cities. His sermons resulted in young people abstaining from drugs, alcohol and trimming their hair (all tenants of the Sikh faith). Tavleen Singh the prominent journalist said his philosophy could be summed up in six words of, *'Nashey shaddo, Amrit Shako, Gursikh*

---

[53] Vaisakhi is the first day of the Sikh month that falls between April & May, the date is usually 13/14th April. It also celebrates the day in 1699 when the 10th Sikh Guru – Guru Gobind Singh created the Khalsa – the current form of initiation for Sikhs.
[54] Many more were injured on the day.
[55] The President of the All India Sikh Students Federation who fought alongside Bhindranwale in the attack on the Harmander Sahib (also known as the Golden Temple) in June 1984
[56] Those of the Indian state of Punjab – both Sikhs and Hindus
[57] G.S Chawla, Assassination of Lala Jagat Narain, Illustrated Weekly of India, October 4, 1981, page 16. Narain was the proprietor of newspapers & was very critical of Bhindranwale & the Dharam Yudh Morcha.

Bano,' (give up addictions, become initiated and disciplined Sikhs).[58]

He talked of his own mission in the following way, *"My mission is to administer Amrit, to explain the meanings of Gurbani and to teach Gurbani to those around me and to tell people that a Hindu should be a firm Hindu, a Muslim should be a firm Muslim and a Sikh should be a firm Sikh*[59]*."*

He was a social reformer who was increasingly growing in fame and support, at the grassroots of Sikh masses. His messages were simple but very effective. He was honest, straight talking and very charismatic. This side of a peaceful preacher is rarely delved into and nor are his religious discourses, which are profound and inspirational.

Many commentators argue he had little formal education, implying he was not very intelligent – but the fact remains that he never came worse off in any interviews with the press, thus what he lacked in formal qualifications, he made up for in other areas of his intelligence. Also, he wasn't an educational drop out but rather chose to concentrate on his spiritual development. He conveyed his messages in a determined and inspirational manner and his religious discourses are amongst the heavyweights of Sikh Scholarly.

Courting Arrest & Dharam Yudh Morcha

After the assassinations of the Nirankari cult leader Gurbachan in 1980[60] and Lala Jagat Narain in 1981[61],

---

[58] Tavleen Singh, Terrorists in the Temple, in: *The Punjab Story*, edited by Amarjit Kaur et al., (1984: 33) Roli Books, , page 33.
[59] Sant Jarnail Singh Bhindranwale, Interview dated February 22, 1984 with a family visiting from Canada, quoted from Sandhu (1999: 376*) Struggle for Justice, Speeches and Conversations of Sant Jarnail Singh Bhindranwale,* Ohio
[60] He was gunned down on 24th April 1980

Bhindranwale became a regular feature in the Punjabi and national press. The killings of both were linked to Bhindranwale and his loyalists but never proven in court.[62]

Arrest warrants for Bhindranwale were made and the Haryana Police attempted to arrest him at Chando Kalan, but he had already left. Thus, he courted arrest voluntarily at an agreed date, in order to be questioned about the Narain killing and was subsequently released one month later. However, Bhai Amrik Singh (AISSF[63]) and Baba Thara Singh[64] were also subsequently arrested in the proceedings. This resulted in the commencement of peaceful civil disobedience protests to achieve the freedom of these two Sikhs who were unlawfully arrested and detained[65]. These two Sikhs were released after peaceful civil disobedience protests, which demonstrated that this method was successful.

The Shromani Akali Dal[66] led by Sant Harchand Singh Longowal was at the time campaigning for the realisation of the Anandpur Sahib Resolution[67] and subsequently implemented the same methods of peacefully protesting and termed this new movement the 'Dharam Yudh Morch' (meaning campaign for righteousness). Bhindranwale grew more in stature as the Morcha rolled forward as He and Longowal were seen to be leading it.

---

[61] He was the owner of Hind Samachar group – which owns a number of newspapers including 'Jag Baani' a popular Punjabi daily. He was an outspoken critic of the Sikhs and was known for using vulgar language against the Sikhs

[62] Although Bhai Ranjit Singh was convicted in the murder case of Gurbachan, no evidence to link Bhindranwale to the assassination was uncovered.

[63] AISSF = All India Sikh Students Federation. This organisation was a radical student/youth organisation that had grassroots support. It was very influential in being able to draw mass support from students across India

[64] Another close confidant of Bhindranwale

[65] No evidence linked them to the crime, yet their detention continued unabated

[66] The Leading Sikh Political Party

[67] See Appendix 1

However, Bhindranwale reiterated on a number of occasions that Longowal was the Morcha dictator.

Bhindranwale inspired the masses to court arrest through his speeches and preaching tours, and the masses were accessed via the network of support of the All India Sikh Students Federation led by Bhai Amrik Singh. A gridlock ensued with talks breaking down between the Akalis and the then Prime Minister Indira Gandhi, who purposely manoeuvred away from reaching a compromise. What followed was a fist of iron, aimed at crushing the movement of civil disobedience in 1984 and the proceeding years thereafter.

Why was Bhindranwale fighting for secession/Khalistan?
We regularly hear the following views being expressed on Bhindranwale:

- *"Bhindranwale was a separatist."*

- *"Bhindranwale and his followers were fighting for a Sikh homeland."*

- *"The militants who fortified the Harmander Sahib (Golden Temple) were fighting for Khalistan"*

The above statements are read with some dismay, as repetition of a lie does not make it a fact. Many have fallen prey to these lies and provide no evidence to support these allegations.

Now, the world has moved on considerably since 1984. The internet has exploded and globalization has made the world into a village – whereby facts and information from one part of the planet can be received and relayed in a matter of seconds. Long gone are the days of one single TV channel in India[68] or controlling the mass media with ease. Although, powerful individuals and governments can still wield considerable clout; investigative journalism and social media has meant the truth can prevail or one can find the truth if one searches for the evidence.

All of Bhindranwale's known public speeches and a considerable number of his interviews can be found on the internet[69] and in Ranbir Singh Sandhu's book, "Struggle for Justice",[70] in which the author has meticulously translated a collection of speeches and interviews of Bhindranwale. The following conclusions can be reached after studying the words of Bhindranwale:

1) He fought for more freedom for Punjabis and Sikhs under a true federal system within the union of India as encapsulated in the Anandpur Sahib Resolution;
2) In 1983 Bhindranwale made it clear, 'that the day the Indian Government attacks Harmander Sahib the foundation stone for Khalistan will be laid.' In reality, this would be after June 1984 – not before;
3) In an interview Bhindranwale confirmed his view of Khalistan saying, "I am neither for it nor against it ... If you give it us we will take it." Now this denotes a person in favour of Khalistan but also a person who is clearly unwilling to make it a demand or part of his campaign/movement.

---

[68] In 1984 the only channel was the government controlled Doordarshan, thus the Indian masses only knew what they were told on a general level
[69] http://www.gurmatveechar.com/audio.php?q=f&f=%2FKatha%2F01_Puratan_Katha%2FSant_Jarnail_Singh_%28Bhindran_wale%29%2FSpeeches
[70] Sandhu, R. S. (1999), "Struggle for Justice, Speeches of and Conversations of Sant Jarnail Singh Bhindranwale," Sikh Educational and Religious Foundation, Ohio

So where does this perpetual lie – that Bhindranwale and his followers were fighting for a separate Sikh State stem from? It is a lie that continues to be spouted at every opportunity when the events of 1984 are discussed. I humbly request those that make this claim, to provide any primary evidence to substantiate this claim; from Bhindranwale's words, as I have searched high and low for any shred of evidence to substantiate it and found nothing. I have listened to his words, read them, met and socialised with his surviving friends, family and close confidants and still came up with no proof. I sincerely ask anyone reading this to provide some proof for this claim. Until I see the evidence – I will remain steadfast in my view, that this is quite simply a perpetual lie.

Why did Bhindranwake fortify Harmander Sahib in 1984?

Now, moving on to this more controversial aspect of Bhindranwale; he is accused of fortifying the Gurdwara complex and running a den of criminality from there. This accusation is given as a pre-text to conducting Operation Blue Star[71] by the Indian Army and government. The actual fortifications and what really occurred will be discussed in a later chapter. Here, I will concentrate on the reasons for why Bhindranwale and his associates actually engaged in combat with the army from within the Amritsar Gurdwara complex. These reasons are based on prophecy, destiny, Sikh History and Sikh Approval.

Combat within the Amritsar Gurdwara complex

The first leader of Damdami Taksal, Baba Deep Singh, was martyred freeing Harmander Sahib from its occupation by invaders in 1757 and the second leader of the Taksal, Baba Gurbaksh Singh, was similarly martyred

---

[71] The name given to the attack on Harmander Sahib by the Indian Army, the Blue Star they were aiming at eliminating was Bhindranwale

freeing Harmander Sahib from its occupation by Ahmed Shah Abdali's army in 1765. Historically, invaders and those opposing the Sikhs have always attacked and occupied Harmander Sahib. Now, 30 years on, most Sikhs see Bhindranwale in a similar light – a Sikh who defended Harmander Sahib against an opposing state, who wanted to occupy it.

Therefore, the attack for many Sikhs is a continuum of Sikh History, in which those out to silence the Sikhs or eliminate them, attack Harmander Sahib. Defending it, is strongly ethically based – in that raising arms to defend it, is seen as a moral duty for the Sikhs. In 1984, these Sikh defenders only opened fire on the 3rd June 1984, once the army entered the Gurdwara precincts, even though firing from outside by the security forces had started on the 1st June 1984. The Indian Army were victorious in occupying Harmander Sahib, but they felt the subsequent repercussions afterwards, in the civil war that ensued.

The highest temporal authority for Sikhs or the Sikh Parliament is the Akaal Takhat (timeless throne) which is opposite the Harmander Sahib in the Amritsar complex. The leader (Jathedar) of the Akaal Takhat is seen as the most powerful individual in Sikh polity; he can pass edicts for the Sikh Nation when in conclave with four other Sikhs. Hence, five of them in total can pass these edicts depicting the 'Panj Pyare[72]' (five beloved Sikhs) who can officiate Sikh affairs.

---

[72] The Five Beloved Ones were originally selected when they offered their heads for sacrifice to Guru Gobind Singh in 1699 and were eventually initiated into the Khalsa Nation – having to wear 5 articles of faith and abstaining from alcohol, meat, tobacco, relationships outside of marriage and trimming ones hair. The Five Beloved Ones after being initiated in turn initiated Guru Gobind Singh and today the initiation is still officiated by Five Sikhs representing these Five Beloved Ones. Wherever Five Sikhs who are of high moral living congregate they can officiate on matters of Sikhs (on a local level). The conclave that includes the Akaal Takhat Leader is seen as supreme and can officiate on matters of the whole Sikh nation, wherever the Sikhs may reside.

On the 2nd June 1984, the then Akaal Takhat Jathedar/Leader Giani[73] Kirpal Singh passed an edict stating, *"Keeping in view the unprovoked attack on the Golden Temple, we appeal to all organisations of the Khalsa Panth to defeat the sinister designs of the demoniac forces and repulse the attacks of the C.R.P.F.[74] and B.S.F.[75] to uphold the sanctity of Sri Darbar Sahib, Golden Temple."*[76] The full edict can be read at Appendix 3. It is clear from the edict that Sikhs are being ordered to raise arms and defend the complex. Therefore, Bhindranwale was actually mandated to defend the complex and repulse the attack, as were all Sikhs. The only reason that many Sikhs did not learn of this edict was due to the excessive press censorship and government actions to suppress such information from reaching the masses.

Many argue that Bhindranwale could have avoided unnecessary blood-shed by vacating the complex, but this ignores the fact of excessive force used by the army and the very poignant fact that at least 42 other Gurdwara's were simultaneously attacked[77]. This essentially leads us to the conclusion that the attack on Harmander Sahib - was in one aspect, an assault on the Sikhs.

Bhindranwale & pre-1984
Turning to the politics pre-dating 1984. Some argue that Bhindranwale was an agent of the Congress Party,[78] they cite this as a reason as to how he avoided arrest and

---

[73] Giani means learned
[74] Central Reserve Police Force – an armed unit of the police
[75] Border Security Force – due to Amritsar falling within very close proximity of the border, this force was used to attack Harmander Sahib
[76] Upto the 2nd June, 1984 the CRPF and BSF shot at pilgrims and the complex, from 3rd June 1984 the army started their full frontal attack
[77] P. 51, Government White Paper on 1984
[78] Kuldip Nayar, *"How Congress invented a 'Sant'"* in Mail Today, New Delhi, 8 July 2012

detention prior to 1984; only being arrested once and subsequently released[79]. This prompts the question - if he had courted arrest in 1981, why would he not do it again? However, it is important to note that no arrest warrants were produced in June 1984 to apprehend Bhindranwale or the other alleged 'Sikh Militants' in the Harmander Sahib Complex.

If we are to be believe that Bhindranwale was an agent of the Congress, then the argument given is that he was a pawn used by Indira Gandhi to create moral strife amongst the Sikhs. However this 'moral strife' led to both of their deaths. The other argument given is that Bhindranwale was a pawn used by the Congress to split the Sikh vote and in turn get the Congress assured power in Punjab and nationally. The Congress may have benefited communally with this ploy but in Punjab it led to much dislike of them. Also, what is never elaborated upon is – what did Bhindranwale gain from this 'alleged' alignment? He was an honest leader and did not enter power politics and was singularly focussed upon his agenda of reform; to propagate Sikhism, promote their martial spirit, and seek equality and justice for Sikhs.

The more profound point is found when one studies Sant Kartar Singh, who actually organised mass protests against the repressive regime of Indira Gandhi when she called a state of emergency in 1975. Here, it needs to be noted that 37 protest marches were organised with mass involvement, hence Taksal was already at logger heads with Indira Gandhi prior to Bhindranwale's tenure.

Could Indira Gandhi have approached Bhindranwale to work in partnership? Yes, but what would constitute this

---

[79] Arrested in September 1981 and released in October 1981

partnership? What would have been their aims? Other than hearsay and political intrigue, no coherent argument for this alleged partnership is forthcoming. Many do, however, argue that Indira Gandhi engineered the situation in such a way to create a moral panic against the Sikhs; in order to attempt to crush them, and electioneer herself once again as the saviour of India – as she did with the war with Pakistan (that led to the creation of Bangladesh in 1971).

As part of the political engineering, there was a creation of moral panics in the national media of a 'Sikh' threat to national security. Allegations of extortion rackets and criminal activity were rife. Bhindranwale himself describes such attempts to malign his character, *"I like to make an appeal to the congregation and I like to inform the newspapermen too that they can definitely publish it. I have this letter in my hand. Seven such letters that have been received in the Qadian area. One has reached Pritam Singh Bhatia. In that letter too, it is written about a Hindu, that he should reach such and such place, near the railway tracks, where Bhatia Sahib's shelter is located, on August 12th 1983, with 50,000 rupees. The person to whom that letter is addressed has been asked to reach there at such and such time, with 50,000 rupees and if he does not reach there, he should make preparations because he would be finished off in a few days. On the top is written: "There is one God, Eternal: Long live Khalistan." At the end, at the bottom is written: "Long live Bhindranwale.*[80]*"*

Now the above portrays Bhindranwale's audacity and fearfulness. He openly described such attempts to

---

[80] Sant Jarnail Singh Bhindranwale, Speech on August 10, 1983. (quoted from "Struggle for Justice, Speeches and Conversations of Sant Jarnail Singh Bhindranwale," by Ranbir Singh Sandhu 1999, Ohio

assassinate his character and repeatedly asked for evidence, for allegations made against him.

Hindus & Bhindranwale

Bhindranwale was falsely portrayed as a fanatic and racist, who was allegedly determined to destroy the unity of India. It was argued that he wanted Hindus to leave Punjab. To the contrary Bhindranwale actually helped Hindu families, which is aptly described here, *'On a later visit to Amritsar I got an inkling into the reasons of Bhindranwale's popularity. I will narrate two incidents to illustrate this. One day a young girl came to see Bhindranwale, she clutched his feet and sobbed out her story of how she was maltreated by her husband's family for failing to extract more money from her parents and of her husband's unwillingness to take her side. Bhindranwale asked her name and where she lived. "So you are the daughter of the Hindus, he said. "Are you willing to become the daughter of a Sikh?" She nodded. Bhindranwale sent a couple of his armed guards to fetch the girl's family. An hour later, a very frightened trio consisting of the girl's husband and his parents were brought into his presence. "Is this girl a daughter of your household." he demanded. They admitted she was. "She tells me that you want money from her father. I am her father." He placed a tray full of currency notes before them and told them: "take whatever you want". The three fell at his feet and craved forgiveness.*[81]

His closest confidants, Bhai Amrik Singh (AISSF) and Baba Thara Singh built a Mandir – a Hindu temple whilst in prison, so that the Hindu prisoners could offer prayers. Furthermore, Bhindranwale describes financial

---

[81] Nayar & Singh, (1984: 23) *Tragedy of Punjab,* Vision Books, New Delhi,

spend for Hindus in litigation and support for Hindu families;

"In Kapurthula, a copy of the Ramayana was burnt (a Hindu Scripture). The leaders of that place know about this. The Jatha spent 5,000 rupess in litigation over that. On the 4th April 1983, two Hindus were martyred in connection with the 'rasta roko' agitation (road block protest). Shiromoni Akali Dal and the Shromani Committee paid (their families) 10,000 rupees each and the Jatha (the Taksal) gave another 5,000 to each family. If I was an enemy of all the Hindus, where is the need for me to pay all this money?[82]"

The Firebrand Leader

Bhindranwale strongly condemned the killings of innocent people and the bombings that took place throughout Delhi when he was arrested. It has to be accepted that he did make some volatile statements arguing that the Sikhs, if asked to, can each fight 125,000[83]. Thus, if a war were to break ou,t Sikhs could still be victorious in India. He also made other firebrand statements in speeches at times in response to the oppression against Sikhs. Now, it was only these fiery statements purposely taken out of context that were quoted in the national press. A war of attrition raged in the mass media – but you, the readers need to decide how you can go on to conclude the rights and wrongs after an assessment of the facts.

To conclude this chapter on Bhindranwale – we need to consider, whether he was a Saint, an extremist, a revolutionary or a terrorist.

---

[82] Sant Jarnail Singh Bhindranwale, Speech on September 20, 1983. (quoted from "Struggle for Justice, Speeches and Conversations of Sant Jarnail Singh Bhindranwale," by Ranbir Singh Sandhu (1999), Ohio

[83] This statement is in reference to an edict of Guru Gobind Singh, that His Sikhs, will each be able to fight 125,000 combatants

Was he a Saint?

By appointment of Damdami Taksal, yes he was. Was he of profound spirituality and charisma? After studying his religious discourses, life and times, my answer would be in the affirmative. Some would counter this assertion by saying Saints do not engage in acts of violence. However, anyone with a minute knowledge of the Sikh faith would know that Sikhism from its onset has been a revolutionary faith, which has had to raise arms to defend its survival as a race. So yes, he used violence in his defence of Harmander Sahib in 1984 against an invading force, as had leaders of the Taksal prior to him.

There are allegations that Bhindranwale's men carried out assassinations prior to 1984. Bhindranwale was made out to be leading these assassinations by the media and Indian government. He did make volatile statements at times which were then misconstrued to add weight to this image of a leader of a violent campaign against critics and enemies of the Sikhs.

Assassinations did take place between 1978 to 1984 Babbar Khalsa and Dashmesh Regiment[84] were taking responsibility for some of the acts of violence. Dal Khalsa[85] also participated in other criminal acts. Bhindranwale reiterated his stance against many of these acts of violence by immediately condemning them.

The aforementioned organisations operated independently of Bhindranwale and whilst they shared similar goals, they did not share similar methods. The

---

[84] These were both groups who had taken responsibility for assassinations, they were clandestinely run.
[85] An organisation that propagated Khalistan very early on, its members hijacked planes and engaged in political activities.

allegations against Bhindranwale being the figure-head of a campaign of violence were never substantiated and nor was the allegation that he called these hits. It was alleged that he had a hit list and ordered assassinations, his response to this allegation to Indira Gandhi was,

'Upon my life and upon my breath, let her prove where did I get that paper for that hit list, where did I get the pen, the ink and the ink pot. She should get the CBI[86] to check this out. If she proves that I have signed any paper and that I have signed for the purpose of any bodies being killed; standing here in the presence of Hazoor (Guru Granth Sahib), I declare that I shall cut off my head and place it before the congregation. I shall leave Guru Nanak Niwas and go away.'[87]

Was he an extremist?

"Sant Bhindranwale's name was linked with all anti-national and anti-social activities ... The term 'extremism' came to be used almost as a synonym for Sant Bhindranwale's stance and every 'extremist' was identified as his man. Even routine crimes were attributed to the extremists."[88]

The word extremist is a politicised term – it implies someone is extreme in her/his views and that this extreme nature becomes threatening. The simple answer is yes, he was unflinching in the demands that he supported as part of the Dharam Yudh Morhca. He did not waiver, or change his view, as do, many political leaders. These traits can be seen as positive and represent an honest and consistent view.

---

[86] Central Bureau of Investigation
[87] Sant Jarnail Singh Bhindranwale, speech on 16 October 1983 (can be seen at Sandhu (1999: 293) *Struggle for Justice, Speeches and Conversations of Sant Jarnail Singh Bhindranwale,* Ohio
[88] Kaur (2006: 68), Blue Star Over Amritsar, Corporate Vision, New Delhi

If one were to say, 'I think the Pope or the Dalai Lama is an extremist' – many would protest, but the argument can be made, that they are similarly extreme in their views and do not compromise. Therefore, if this is the sort of extremist that people want to label him as, then yes, he was extreme and unflinching in his ideology. This is what he had to say himself,

"One who takes Amrit and helps others take it; who reads the Gurbani (Sikh Scriptires) and teaches others to do the same; who gives up intoxicants and helps others to do likewise; who urges all to get together and work in cooperation; who preaches Hindu-Sikh unity and asks for peaceful coexistence; who says: 'If you are a Muslim, than be a devout Muslim, if you are a Sikh, respect your Isht (Guru Granth Sahib), unite under the saffron Nishaan Sahib (the Sikh Flag) stoutly support the Sikh nation and be attached to Satguru's Throne and Guru's Darbar:" Persons who preach like this are now all being called extremists by this Government and by the Mahasha Press (Right Wing Hindu Press). In particular, I have been given big title. They call me the "leader of the extremists." I am a firm extremist, but of the type which has the characteristic I have described to you[89].'

Joyce Pettigrew describes Bhindranwale in appreciative manner and adds a Western analysis to what he represented, saying he *"... had wished religious values to be placed at the cente of life .. in the democratic societies of the West, these values would not be termed*

---

[89] Sant Jarnail Singh Bhindranwale, speech on May 11, 1983; also interview, with Surinderjit Singh of Vancouver, in January 1983, quoted from "Struggle for Justice, Speeches and Conversations of Sant Jarnail Singh Bhindranwale," by Ranbir Singh Sandhu 1999, Ohio

religious but rather would be described as civil libertarian and socialist."[90]

Was he a terrorist?

A terrorist is somebody who instils fear in people through actions which are usually outlawed by a nation state. However, Bhindranwale was never found guilty of any crime.
Yes, he fought against the Indian Army in the June 1984 attack, but prior to that, no acts of crime can be confirmed and as argued above, he had a mandate to defend the Harmander Sahib as did every Sikh, from the Akaal Takhat edict of 2nd June 1984. The Indian state waged war against the Sikhs in Harmander Sahib – so the debate will rage on, of who were the real terrorists? Was it the less than 200 fighters aligned with Bhindranwale? Or was it the Indian state?

I do not view him as a terrorist, as his actions do not in my view amount to terrorism. He courted arrest once, when criminal investigations were pending, and was released unconditionally. Prior to Operation Blue Star no criminal charges were levelled against him and even until today – the Indian government has not provided any evidence of his so-called "terrorism." Yes, they have him on audio giving a few fiery speeches, which are publically available, but other than that, no incriminating evidence is ever presented to substantiate the accusations of "terrorism." If delivering fiery speeches makes him a terrorist, then there are definitely a lot of terrorists in the world.

Thirty years on – we need to study the facts, and draw our own conclusions; rather than simply believe a

---

[90] Pettigrew (1995: 55), *The Sikhs of the Punjab*, Zed Books, London

view espoused without evidence. Bhindranwale's life and times have been recorded, his recordings can all be found on www.gurmatveechar.com and Sandhu's book[91] translates into English nearly every known recording of Bhindranwale. Cross-referencing the allegations against him is now possible and can become empirical. Please study these sources to gain a real view of the man.

Was he a revolutionary?

He started a mass revival of Sikhism whereby 500 people began to become initiated every Wednesday and Sunday at the Akaal Takhat. At one such initiation ceremeony 10,000 were initiated. Bhindranwale himself highlighted this phenomenon on 19th April 1984,

"Over the last twenty to thirty years there have never been more than three hundred persons prepared to receive Amrit at Siri Akaal Takhat Sahib; in twenty years! Now every Wednesday and Sunday, four hundred to four hundred and fifty persons, and even up to five hundred persons receive Amrit ... During the month of Chet (mid-March to mid-April), your Jatha has administered Amrit to 45,000 persons in just one month."

This religious revival was backed by the AISSF and became a national revolution in halting apostasy amongst Sikhs.

The Akaal Takhat Jathedar[92] Bhai Joginder Singh Vedanti awarded Bhindranwale with the honorific title of, the "Greatest Sikh of the 20th Century" in 2007[93]. It took

---

[91] "Struggle for Justice, Speeches and Conversations of Sant Jarnail Singh Bhindranwale," by Ranbir Singh Sandhu 1999, Ohio

[92] High Priest – Leader of temporal matters for Sikhs

[93] http://www.dnaindia.com/india/report-bhindranwale-greatest-sikh-warrior-of-the-20th-century-1136513 This news story refers to the installation of the photo of Bhindranwale in the Sikh Museum.

over 20 years for the moderate leadership of the Sikhs to take this stance and it was taken under popular pressure to reflect the feelings amongst Sikhs. Many moderate Sikhs had been critical of Bhindranwale and fell foul to the mass media image that was promoted by the government prior to 1984 and the years that followed, but now the tide has clearly turned.

A memorial has now been raised in the Harmander Sahib complex to commemorate those who defended it, against the Indian army. His photo hangs in the museum of Harmander Sahib as it does in homes, Gurdwaras and cars throughout the globe. Anywhere his photo is printed becomes an instant money spinner, be it on t-shirts, posters, or memorabilia – he is the iconic Sikh Hero. His speeches and discourses are listened to and revered. So does he represent a revolutionary leader of the Sikhs? All of the aforementioned points would lead us to say yes – what 'Che Guevera' represents for the Cubans, Bhindranwale is for the Sikhs.

1984

This "holocaust" of 1984 is bound to reverberate through Sikh history for a long time to come.
Cynthia Mahmood (1996:73)

The frenzy and bogey of alleged 'Sikh' terrorism, fanaticism and extremism had been set rolling on its destructive path. The Congress government were playing power politics and their own Chief Minister Darbara Singh resigned from his post, citing a law and order situation that he could no longer maintain. This cleared the path for Presidents rule to be imposed in Punjab, in October 1983, allowing rule from the centre.

Punjab was one of India's most important states, its river waters irrigated vital lands in other states and generated power; its paddy yield made it India's breadbasket. Punjab neighboured Pakistan, which meant it had to be guarded at all times from possible invasions and warfare. Punjab was and still is of strategic importance to India.

The Sikh leaders taking refuge in Harimander Sahib had allegedly become confrontational and were co-ordinating terrorism from within the Gurdwara precinct[94]. Assassinations were taking place throughout Punjab and Sikhs were brandishing firearms. Bhindranwale had urged Sikhs to become armed and this had been one of the demands of the Anandpur Sahib Resolution; that Sikhs be permitted to bear arms without a license.

Bhindranwale was spurring on the Sikh youth to take to arms and deliver 'Sikh' justice if the methods of Daleel (reason), Vakeel (via the law and lawyers) and appeal

---
[94] Indian Government White Paper on Punjab Agitation, July 1984

(appealing against unjust judgements and winning) bore no fruit. A defence of one's own honour and that of the Guru and Sikh Nation was propagated; historical examples of Sikhs doing this were mixed with fiery speeches. The security forces of India were forever getting more frustrated with law and order, resulting in them becoming directly involved by killing peaceful protestors and taking it upon themselves to avenge the lives of those who were assassinated. A communal undertone was started through the media and misrepresentation of the issues made.

The Hindu Right Wing played its part in attacking the Sikh faith and supporting the view that Sikhs were hell bent on destroying the integrity of India. They supported sects such as the Nirankaris who were declared heretical by the Sikhs[95]. *"There is no doubt that Lala Jagat Narains papers played a role in fanning the flames of communal hatred between Hindus and Sikhs."*[96] Editorials were usually themed about the support for Khalistan by Sikhs and that the government needs to take stringent action.[97]

This all led to 1984 – the year of the beginning of the politics of genocide for the Sikhs. The events still reverberate in homes, law courts and parliaments across the globe. Four events would define this year – Operation Blue Star, Operation Woodrose, Indira Gandhi's assassination and the anti-Sikh pogroms that followed.

Attack on Harmander Sahib, Amritsar

---

[95] On the 10th June 1978 an edict from Akaal Takhat was passed declaring that all Sikhs must cease all ties with Nirankaris and those that do not, will be outcast from the community

[96] Tully & Jacob, (2006:66) *Amritsar Mrs Gandhi's Last Battle,* Rupa & Co, New Delhi. Lala Jagat Narain owned the Hind Samachar Group, which owned newspapers and was a media conglomerate. It played a pivotal role in inflaming issues.

[97] ibid

Now let us turn our attention back to the Army Operation to flush out alleged 'terrorists' from Harmander Sahib in Amritsar. Events were escalating to this tumultuous eventuality and on the 15th December 1984, Bhindranwale moved his residence from Nanak Niwas (a residential quarter of the complex) to a building adjoining the Akaal Takhat. It would be from here that the strategic command of an ex-Indian Army General, Subegh Singh, would lead to a bloody battle with Indian Army personnel. From here, Bhindranwale would fight with his associates until the 6th June 1984, defending and preventing occupation by the Army from the 3rd June 1984.

A comparison with the recent Iraq war would be pertinent at this point. The USA and UK governments went to war with Iraq, on the basis of Saddam Hussain amassing weapons of mass destruction. After the war was won and lost, it transpired that there were actually no weapons of mass destruction and they simply never existed. It was pure fabrication. A similar case can be said to exist when analysing the situation of the Sikhs in 1984. Pure fabrication of fake threats to peace and reasons for army assaults, that did not add up.

The Indian Government White Paper maintains that it was the lawlessness in Punjab, that led to the army operation and it was necessary, to control the problem of growing terrorism. However, the White Paper fails to disclose any details of who these terrorists were? Or any list of offences that these individuals had supposedly committed? If these terrorists were causing so much havoc across Punjab and India, and the government knew who they were, surely a list could have been produced in the White Paper, along with a charge sheet and arrest warrants for these allegedly 'wanted terrorists.' Nothing of such kind exists – but we are supposed to believe the accusations levelled at those who were living in Harmander Sahib at the time of the army assault. Guilt was already proven as far as the Indian government was concerned and no further proof was required.

The White Paper on pages 110 – 162 does however, give a detailed list of violent incidents throughout Punjab between the years of 1981 – 1984, it provides no details on the identity of the suspected offenders and their associations with 'Sikh terrorism' or 'Bhindranwale'. Thus, it is accepted that these incidents could have occurred, but what links they had with the spectre of 'Sikh terrorism' still needs empirically verifying.

The Government White Paper still remains a conflicting document when studying the events of 1984. It is at complete odds with eye-witness accounts and independent research by respected Hindus who wanted to unearth the truth. These brave Hindus went out and risked their own lives in an atmosphere of state oppression and most of them were later charged with sedition, when they published their findings.

One book that contains independent eye witness accounts is 'Oppression in Punjab' by an organisation called, 'Citizens for Democracy.'[98] They published their findings in the book in 1985 and it was immediately banned in India and still is. The authors were arrested and charged under a number of oppressive laws[99]. The foreword to the book was written by Justice Tarkunde (1909 – 2004) who was himself a left wing Congress party member of old. The book was, however, republished

---

[98] The book can be viewed at http://www.shaheed-khalsa.com/oip.html
[99] On Spetember 10, 1985 all the five researchers were arrested and charged with crimes under the National Security Act, Armed Forces Special Powers Act 1983 and Terrorists and Disruptive Activities Act 1985.

clandestinely and widely distributed in India, UK, Canada and USA.

My research for this book also included interviewing a number of survivors of Operation Blue Star. This includes an array of combatants and innocent pilgrims who were trapped inside the complex. I also have friends in Amritsar who lived through this period and witnessed the excesses of it. Thus, I have studied sources and had interviews with a number of eye witnesses. I have attempted to be as balanced as I could in my research for this book.

Unravelling the truth

The problem we face in the empiricism of the study of these events is that we have two completely different accounts of what really occurred. The Indian Government view or what may be referred to as the 'official' view, which includes the army, press, radio, tv and white paper of 1984, which in effect all say mostly the same thing(s). The 'unofficial' view of eye witnesses, independent commentators and that of banned reports/books refer to the whole episode as a planned massacre and the Sikhs refer to it as a 'Ghallughara,' a genocide.

Those that perished in the attack and those persecuted subsequently, have had no or little voice in the matter, for every 100 accounts of the attack, only 1 unofficial account surfaces – thus their accounts have lost credibility. Credit is due to those that did speak up and told the truth in the face of death and persecution.

Attempting to find a balance or middle ground about what really occurred in Operation Blue Star becomes virtually impossible. The 'official' view through its mass media apparatus attempted to completely whitewash the whole issue and deceive the masses of what really happened. Media censorship and restriction of movements in and out of Punjab, meant that the governmental apparatus did it's best to create a singular reporting of the events and this was backed with new acts of legislation and pursuit of those who wrote views counter to this 'official' view.

On a basic cultural level, anyone who has lived in or studied India, will know of the rabid corruption of government officials, thus healthy scepticism about the 'official' view of most things is maintained. These issues in studying these historical events and attempting to ascertain what really happened, has led to much animosity and passionate debates.

I will now start analysing the actual events of Operation Blue Star and hope to paint a picture of what the differing sources argue – thus the readers can then draw their own conclusions of what really occurred.

The build up to Operation Blue Star
On 23rd March 1983, Rajiv Gandhi[100] stated, *"I think we should not enter the Golden Temple. The Police can enter temples, but it is a question of what is good balance. Today as we see it, it is not as if the Sikhs are against the Hindus, and we should do nothing that separates them."*[101] These sentiments were backed by the Deputy Commissioner of Amritsar – Gurdev Singh, who refused to sanction the army entering Harmander Sahib and was relieved of his post on 2nd June 84. He had advised the use of local police as opposed to the army, due to local

---

[100] Son of Indira Gandhi and member of the Congress Party at this point, he would become the Prime Minister after the assassination of his mother
[101] Samiuddin (1985: 227) *The Punjab Crisis: Challenge & Response,* South Asia Books

intelligence of the complex and adjoining buildings that the local administration had. He had argued that the police could extract Bhindranwale and his men with relative ease. He argued calling in the army would be seen as an alien aggression of the Sikh Vatican. His appeals fell on deaf ears.[102]

The white paper explains the official view of why the attack had to take place, *"the government was convinced that this challenge to the security, unity and integrity of the country could not be met by normal law and order agencies at the disposal of the state."*[103] Jaijee points out that the use of the army and calling of a curfew was actually illegal, as no martial law had been enacted.[104]

Similarly General Sinha who was the next in line to become the Chief of the Army and was the Western Army Commander in the 1980's (covering Punjab), had divergent views from the government of the day. He had laid out a specific procedure on how the army should engage in religious shrines, should they need to enter one, in a dispute.

General Sinha frankly speaks about his advice prior to the attack in an interview; had his advice been followed the massacre that took place could have easily been avoided. He says,

"...I had laid down, was that, when the Army is called out, we would do everything in a very transparent manner. We would invite some eminent Sikh gentlemen from Amritsar to come and witness what we are doing so that wrong reports do not come out. Secondly, I would

---

[102] Jaijee, (1999: 68) *Politics of Genocide,* Ajanta Publishing, Delhi
[103] P.3, Indian Government The White Paper on The Punjab Agitation (July 1984)
[104] See pages 68-69 in - Inderjit Singh Jaijee, *Politics of Genocide,* Ajanta Publishing, Delhi (1999)

request TV Coverage of the whole operation, so that the people can see what we are doing. I would have a cordon round Golden Temple established so that no one can go out or come in, and announce to Bhindranwala and his people, we do not want to enter the temple, that is sacrilege for us as it is for you. You come out, give them time, 24 hours, 48 hours, or even more. And in the meanwhile, cut out electricity to them, water supply, to make things difficult and coerce them.

Simultaneously I said, we should have a Sikh Officer commanding the operation, and the mixture of Sikh and non-Sikh troops. We should get a temporary Gurdwara established outside with a cordon, where we should offer prayers. Let the whole thing be resolved peacefully and the Army not forced to enter the Gurdwara. If in spite of all that he doesn't respond and we have to go in, then all troops taking part in the operations should offer prayers at our temporary Gurdwara before going in, have ensured that their heads are covered and take off their shoes, go barefoot. And when you enter, use minimum force and try and get the better of them."[105]

This protocol was ignored and the government instead chose to forge ahead with its own idea. General Sinha was side-stepped for his promotion to become the Chief of the Army, something that General Vaidiya achieved, by leading Operation Blue Star and appeasing Indira Gandhi.

The Punjab had been under President's rule and the Amritsar complex of Harmander Sahib was guarded, and all things going in and out were searched. The Central Reserve Police Force (CRPF) and Border Security Force

---

[105] The interview with Day & Night News can be viewed at http://www.youtube.com/watch?v=db5GX0LLN-4 & relevant parts of the interview can be viewed at Appendix 5

(BSF) had been out in force for months, surrounding the complex. The allegation of fortifications by Sikhs inside and that of Bhindranwale is questionable on a number of grounds. Firstly, thousands visit and pay their respects on a daily basis – so where were the fortifications taking place, as thousands of pilgrims did not notice them. Even if they were taking place clandestinely, Bhindranwale would meet the press almost daily and did not hide from interviews or questioning from visitors – so he was actually quite accessible from within the confines of the complex.

Although, Bhindranwale and his men were armed, that must be acknowledged, as were members of Babbar Khalsa. Arms could have been smuggled into the complex and P.S.Bhinder an Inspector General of Police admitted that trucks carrying provisions for the Langar (free kitchen) were not searched, as he had been ordered from above, to not search them.[106]

Furthermore, the intelligence agencies were all working hand-in-glove with the army to study the so called 'fortifications.' *"Some army officers, including Major-General K.S. Brar ... who was to lead the operation, had gone round the Temple incognito to see the defenders' fortifications."*[107] So if they had seen the fortifications, how did they get the planning so wrong?

The army were resolutely held off for at least 3 days, at the height of a pitched battle. General Sunderji[108] commented afterwards that, to say intelligence was inadequate was the understatement of the year, and that it was virtually non-existent.[109] So we must conclude, that

---
[106] Samiuddin (1985: 230) *The Punjab Crisis: Challenge & Response,* South Asia Books
[107] Kushwant Singh (1991:359), – A History of the Sikhs Vol. 2, Oxford University Press, Delhi
[108] Another General leading Operation Blue Star
[109] Chopra, (1984:27) *Agony of Punjab*, South Asia Books

either the Sikhs who would go on to defend Harmander Sahib fortified the Gurdwara expertly and clandestinely, or that quite simply very little fortifying went on before-hand. The army were caught unawares and were lambs to the slaughter when the offensive began as their intelligence was very poor.

The scene was set and the army operation would go ahead. In October 1983, 600 personnel from the Indian Army had practised the assault on a model at the Chakrata Hills, about 150 miles north of Delhi.[110] The army entered Punjab in large numbers, it is estimated by a number of sources that 70,000 personnel entered Punjab. The actual attack would have 15,000 participating, one commentator added *"... not since the independence has the army been used in such numbers about 15,000 took part in the assault."*[111]

Operation Blue Star

> *Since independence, it was for the first time that the Indian Army had been employed to fight a pitched battle against a section of its own people. The assault on the Golden Temple on 5-6 June 1984 turned a shrine of great sanctity into a battlefield ... The immediate question that arises is: was the army action really necessary? Was it the only solution? My view is that it was not.*
>
> Lt Gen Jagjit Singh Arora, 1984[112]

1st June 1984

---

[110] Mary Anne Weaver, Sunday Times, 17 June 1984
[111] Mary Anne Weaver, Sunday Times, 17 June 1984
[112] In, "The Punjab Story" First published in 1984, 7th impression 2013, page 123

On the 1st June 1984 indiscriminate firing upon the Harmander Sahib complex was commenced by the CRPF from outside. This firing took place between 12.40pm to 8pm, it started with no warning and there was no response from inside the complex.[113] The President of India confirms that firing began without warning, *"Later, I became to know that no such warning had been issued by the authorities and the operation had been suddenly launched."*[114]

The Government White Paper is mysteriously silent about what happened on the 1st June 1984 and rather it starts with events from the 2nd June 1984. All India Radio alsdo announced that unprovoked firing had started from within the complex.

Devinder Singh Duggal, an eye witness who was present throughout the attack and was the librarian of the complex museum, stated that the defenders of the complex were under strict orders from Bhindranwale to not respond to the fire and were only to return fire when the army actually entered. He found this out as he was somewhat dumbfounded by their non-response to the firing that led to 8 deaths, 34 bullet holes in Harmander Sahib, some that were 3 inches wide in diameter.[115]

The curfew was lifted at 8.30pm on 1st June 1984 and people were allowed to enter and leave the complex. This is confirmed by other accounts and one of those who had dead was Bhai Kulwant Singh of the Babbar Khalsa. He was killed by a sniper bullet; he would later go on to be

---

[113] Amiya Rao et al, (1985: 55) *Oppression in Punjab,* Hind Mazdoor Kisan Panchayat Publication by Citizens for Democracy,
[114] Zail Singh (1997:178) *Memories of Giani Zail Singh, The Seventh President of India,* New Delhi,
[115] Amiya Rao et al, (1985:56) *Oppression in Punjab,* Hind Mazdoor Kisan Panchayat Publication by Citizens for Democracy,

cremated in the complex, but only after his parents had been brought to the funeral. There was no firing on the 2nd June 1984.

2nd June 1984

On the 2nd June 1984, Indira Gandhi made an address to the nation through Doordarshan the single national TV channel about the operation; pretending a peaceful solution was still possible. *"She ended the appeal: 'Don't shed blood, shed hatred.' At the time she had already authorised the army to do precisely the opposite: to shed blood which, she ought to have known, would generate hatred of the kind, the country had not experienced since Independence."*[116] On the night of the 2nd June 1984 the CRPF was replaced by the army and all those leaving the complex at night, were arrested and interrogated.

3rd June 1984

The 3rd June was a very significant Sikh commemoration – the fifth Sikh Guru, Guru Arjan Dev, had attained martyrdom peacefully on this day in 1606[117]. Thus, Sikhs from all over the globe would converge at Harmander Sahib for this commemoration, as it was the fifth Guru who had built Harmander Sahib and authored the first compilation of Guru Granth Sahib. About 10,000 pilgrims came to the complex on the 2nd June for this reason. The timing of the attack by the army is highly questionable. Why would the government choose such an important commemoration to launch the attack? Critics of India argue it was chosen to ensure maximum casualties.

---

[116] Kushwant Singh (1991:358), *A History of the Sikhs Vol. 2*, Oxford University Press, Delhi

[117] He was tortured to death and he peacefully endured the torture, accepting God's will. His martyrdom was a result of his rising popularity and the Mughal administration's dislike of the growth of Sikhism and enmity of some government officials.

The Akalis had also planned an agitation for this day, so 1300 volunteers had come in preparation of this peaceful protest. By mid-day on the 2nd June, pilgrims wanting to leave Amritsar via train could not do so, as all the trains were cancelled. Stranded pilgrims thus returned to the Harmander Sahib complex. The pilgrims *"... had been given no inkling or warning either of the sudden curfew or the imminent army attack. It was to be a black-hole type of tragedy, not out of forgetfulness but out of deliberate planning and design."*[118] Furthermore, *"... innocent people were slaughtered like rats, first letting them enter the complex and then declaring the curfew which prevented them from going out, thousands were caught unawares, finally when the survivors were asked to surrender they were shot in cold blood..."*[119]

On the 3rd June 1984, the banning of foreigners from Punjab was enacted through law, as was press censorship.[120] Thus, a black out of any independent reporting commenced, the excuse given in the white paper for this, is that it was done in an attempt to contain communal tensions.

However, Brahma Chellaney of the Associated Press managed to witness some of the atrocities and later reported on them. He found at least 13 people had been killed in cold blood with their hands tied behind their backs (with their turbans) and reported that 200 army officers had died in the attack.[121] He was charged with sedition for his reporting. Who knows what else he might have said, had he not been persecuted.

---

[118] Amiya Rao et al, (1985:58) *Oppression in Punjab*, Hind Mazdoor Kisan Panchayat Publication by Citizens for Democracy
[119] Ibid P.10
[120] P.43-44, Indian Government White Paper on Punjab Agitation, July 1984
[121] Amiya Rao et al, (1985:87) *Oppression in Punjab*, Hind Mazdoor Kisan Panchayat Publication by Citizens for Democracy,

4th June 1984

On the 4th June 1984, bombardment from the army began, with the use of cannon fire, firing of bullets in all directions and the cutting of water and power supply to the complex. Firing would continue unabated until the 6th June 1984[122]. The decision to cut water supply to the complex was a very inhumane strategy to use. We must remember it was the scorching month of June, there were thousands of pilgrims present, up to 20,000 throughout the complex, many would die from the heat and dehydration.

Furthermore, an eye witness, Karnail Kaur stated,*"When people begged for water, some jawans (soldiers) told them to drink the mixture of blood and urine on the ground."*[123] Bhan Singh the secretary of the Gurdwara Committee (SGPC) described the horrid scene, *"Some had to take water out of the drains where dead bodies were lying and the water was red with blood ... The Army people were there, moving about mercilessly without showing any sign of sympathy with those injured or wounded."*[124]

Bhan Singh said no prior warning was given to commencement of firing and no opportunity to leave.[125] Two hymn singers would be killed, whilst performing their duty at Harmander Sahib, Avtar Singh a 65 year old blind devotional singer and Amrik Singh[126]. The government contends that no firing was made upon Darbar Sahib, yet no evidence of any firing from within Harmander Sahib's

---

[122] Amiya Rao et al, (1985:58) *Oppression in Punjab,* Hind Mazdoor Kisan Panchayat Publication by Citizens for Democracy Ibid
[123] Tully & Jacob, (2006: 211) *Amritsar Mrs Gandhi's Last Battle,* Rupa & Co, New Delhi,
[124] Amiya Rao et al, (1985:69) *Oppression in Punjab,* Hind Mazdoor Kisan Panchayat Publication by Citizens for Democracy
[125] ibid P. 59
[126] Ibid P.59

(The actual Golden Temple Gurdwara) was found when searched by the army on 6th June 1984.

5th June 1984

A female student describes the scene on the 5th June, 1984 – she was near the Akaal Takhat and she heard an army announcement for people to surrender. Out of sheer desperation, some people ventured out, as they were thirsty for water – she saw their dead bodies in the walkway (Parikarma) in the morning[127]. The White Paper also agrees that an announcement for surrender was made on the 5th June 1984 – but it contends that 129 people surrendered.[128]

The White Paper claims that the army commenced preliminary actions of clearing buildings to the periphery of the complex on the 5th June 1984 at 1900 hours. It also states that firing from defenders was encountered from the library on the same night, causing a fire to erupt. It says, that despite continued efforts by the army to put the fire out, the library was gutted.[129] Duggal the librarian gives a completely different account – he argues that the library, *"...Guru Nanak Niwas, Teja Singh Samundri Hall, Guru Ram Das Serai and the Langar Buildings had been burnt. When I left the complex on the 6th all these buildings were in good shape in spite of the army attack."*

When Duggal returned to the complex on the 14th June 1984, the library was empty of all its artefacts and gutted with fire damage, and the other buildings were

---

[127] Amiya Rau et al, (1985.62) *Oppression in Punjab*, Hind Mazdoor Kisan Panchayat Publication by Citizens for Democracy
[128] P.48 Indian Government White Paper – Punjab Agitation, July 1984
[129] Ibid

severely damaged.[130] This suggests that the army purposely went on to destroy these buildings; after occupying the Gurdwara. The SGPC[131] – the management committee of most Gurdwaras in Punjab, has had a legal case against the Indian Government lodged in court, about the return of the artefacts from the library, the case is still pending in the legal system, with no end in sight.

To control what the government referred to as a threat to national security, further Gurdwaras were simultaneously attacked. Forty-two religious places were identified where alleged 'terrorists' were based and, on the 5th June 1984, 'terrorists' who didn't surrender were flushed out by the army.[132] Thus, the one point that is consistent within the White Paper and the actions taken, is that alleged Sikh 'terrorists' had taken haven in Gurdwaras across Punjab and that the quickest and most sensible solution, was to attack them, in these Gurdwaras, by the use of the army.

I have shared the figures of alleged 'terrorists' earlier and once again, we must ask where were the charge sheets and the evidence that 'terrorists' had taken haven in these places across Punjab? This is a salient point that the White Paper does not entertain, rather the reader is assumed to just accept the government account, as a given.

6th June 1984

On the 6th June 1984, a relaxation of the curfew was made between 12 noon and 5pm, Harcharan Singh Ragi said he witnessed hundreds of innocent people being shot dead, whilst they came out. He only survived after his

---

[130] Amiya Rao et al, (1985:65-66) *Oppression in Punjab*, Hind Mazdoor Kisan Panchayat Publication by Citizens for Democracy,
[131] Shromani Gurdwara Parbhandak Committee
[132] P.53 Indian Government White Paper – Punjab Agitation, July 1984

daughter showed his I.D. badge of being a Gurdwara employee to the Army Colonel, whilst she begged for their lives.[133]

A female student described how she witnessed four boys being killed by the army. She witnessed the army take off their turbans and tie their hands behind their backs; beating them with rifle butts and shooting them in cold blood whilst accusing them of being terrorists. [134] The greatest insult that one can cause a Sikh is to remove his/her turban, it is similar to knocking off a crown of a monarch, the army knew the offence this would cause.

The White Paper states that 200 terrorists surrendered on 6th June 1984, and that 22 were from within Harmander Sahib.[135] Giani Puran Singh, a Head Priest (Granthi) of the Harmander Sahib, argues that none of the 22 people who surrendered from Harmander Sahib were 'terrorists' and that they were employees of the Gurdwara and some innocent devotees.[136] Giani Kirpal Singh confers with Giani Puran Singh about the identity of these 22 people. He says it was also declared on All India Radio that 22 terrorists had surrendered.[137]

The White Paper in all its lists of terrorists and civilians, counts them continually as one and the same, thus no differentiation was made in how they treated them. This point of not differentiating between combatants and innocent pilgrims in the White Paper is very significant, as it proves that all those captured were treated as criminals.

---

[133] Amiya Rao et al, (1985:69) *Oppression in Punjab,* Hind Mazdoor Kisan Panchayat Publication by Citizens for Democracy,
[134] Ibid P.67
[135] P.50 Indian Government White Paper – Punjab Agitation, July 1984
[136] P.72 Indian Government White Paper – Punjab Agitation, July 1984
[137] Anurag Singh (Translated & Edited), (1999:14) *Giani Kirapl Singh's Eye Witness Account of Operation Blue Star*, B. Chattar Singh Jiwan Singh, Amritsar,

Many of these innocent people couldn't escape after being trapped inside. It proves that the army had no handle on the situation and treated all of them as prisoners of war, which led to the arrest and detention of many of these innocent pilgrims.

On the night of the 6th June at 0100 hours it is argued that Longowal, Tohra (the head of the SGPC) and 350 people surrendered at Nanak Niwas, *"The terrorists opened fire at them and also lobbed hand grenades to prevent their surrender. As a result, seventy people were killed including 39 women and 5 children."*[138] This is very contentious on a number of grounds. Firstly, from all accounts of surviving combatants and even surviving Indian army personnel – the fighting was at its height by this time, and was all centred around capturing the Akaal Takhat. All other areas of the complex had been captured by the army, the remaining fighters were fighting for their lives from within the Akaal Takhat. So, how those fighting the army miraculously got to the opposite side of the complex – is highly dubious, Lieutenant General Arora mirrors these thoughts when writing about this incident.[139]

The eye witness account of Gurmit Singh Cheema needs highlighting here, he saw 800 people massacred by the army. He says, 1000 people were captured and told to sit in lines in Guru Ram Das Serai.[140] At 4.30am grenades were thrown at these people, who had already been searched and disarmed of their Kirpans[141]. They were then subjected to indiscriminate fire. Men, women and children were killed, an estimated 800 died in total.[142]

---

[138] P.49 Indian Government White Paper – Punjab Agitation, July 1984
[139] In, The Punjab Story, 2013, Roli Books, New Delhi
[140] A residential hostel for pilgrims within the complex
[141] Ceremonial swords or daggers – each initiated Sikh wears a Kirpan at all times
[142] Anurag Singh (Translated & Edited), (1999:16-17) *Giani Kirapl Singh's Eye Witness Account of Operation Blue Star*, B. Chattar Singh Jiwan Singh, Amritsar,

Most of the dead bodies recovered after the attack, had hands tied behind their backs, and the dead were found to have been killed in cold blood. Post mortems would later confirm this method of killing, as common amongst the dead, from the complex.[143]

Many also died from their injuries due to negligence of the army in the complex, whilst others died in army camps.[144] The Red Cross were not allowed in to the complex, an unheard of practice in any warfare – clearly demonstrating the army and government had things to hide and were callous in their attitude towards the injured.

The Dead
The White Paper states that the defenders of Harmander Sahib had sophisticated weapons, including anti tank weapons and that an arms factory to make grenades and sten guns, had been set up.[145] There is no other source to verify these claims and eye witnesses have commented that the defending Sikhs fired very sparsely, and had very old weapons.

Lieutenant General J.S. Aurora a veteran of many battles dismissed the claim of sophisticated weapons and said, *"There is, however, the need to correct the picture that has been painted by the media that sophisticated weapons were found inside the Temple ... It is obvious, therefore, that there were not so many sophisticated weapons."*[146] The most likely actuality was that the defenders had a few automatic weapons and, having killed

---

[143] Tully & Jacob, (2006: 176 & 190) *Amritsar Mrs Gandhi's Last Battle,* Rupa & Co, New Delhi,
[144] Amiya Rau et al, (1985: 75) *Oppression in Punjab,* Hind Mazdoor Kisan Panchayat Publication by Citizens for Democracy,
[145] P.51 Indian Government White Paper – Punjab Agitation, July 1984
[146] P.133, The Punjab Story, 2013, Roli Books, New Delhi

incoming soldiers, they then used Indian Army artillery to kill the incoming army.

The defenders had been trained by General Subegh Singh an ex-Indian Army General who had been dishonourably discharged, just before his retirement. He had trained Bangladeshi guerrillas in the war against Pakistan, which led to Bangladeshi independence in 1971. He knew the tactics the Indian army would employ and made good use of his experience, training the Sikhs defending the complex.

The White paper lists the casualties as:

1. Own troops killed   83
2. Troops wounded   249
3. Civilians/terrorists killed   493
4. Terrorists/others injured   86
5. Terrorists/civilians apprehended   592

The White Paper has clearly downplayed the casualties and from my own independent research with survivors of the Operation, I have learnt that there were only about 200 defenders. From this 200, between 60 - 85 were killed in combat and the rest were either arrested, injured or escaped from the complex (on the night of the 5th June 1984 or before).

The list of the known defenders who were felled, can be seen at the end of the museum in Harmander Sahib, where their names are inscribed. The actual fatalities were definitely in excess of 1500 and up to a maximum of 7000. Rajiv Gandhi has been widely quoted as stating that 700 army officers died in the operation, even though he later denied the comment. Kushwant Singh puts the figure of the dead in excess of 5000[147] and Ved Marwah puts it down to a very precise 4712.[148]

The Indian Government in its haste after Operation Blue Star; speedily reconstructed a new Akaal Takhat building. The Sikhs later tore down this state-sponsored reconstruction of the Akaal Takhat and rebuilt the Akaal Takhat themselves, which is the current building for the Gurdwara.

Repercussions

To add insult to injury – the government started to relay Kirtan (hymn singing) from Harmander Sahib on 8th June 1984, on All India Radio. This had been agreed in February 1984, but was purposely commenced after Blue Star to try to appease the Sikhs and white wash the atrocities. This backfired as the Head Priests told the Kirtani's (hymn singers) to sing verses about oppression, at the times of broadcast from 4.30am to 6am and 5pm to 5.30pm.[149]

Leading moderates and pro-Congress party members were also incensed by the army action, leading to Captain Amarinder Singh quitting the Congress Party, the author Kushwant Singh (1915 – 2014)[150] returning awards from the government, as did Bhagat Puran Singh (1904 – 1992)[151] of Pingalwara and many others.[152]

---

[147] Kushwant Singh in Harminder Kaur, (2006: xiv) *Blue Star Over Amritsar,* Corporate Vision, , New Delhi
[148] Ved Marwah, *Uncivil Wars: Pathology of Terrorism in India,* South Asia Book, Delhi, (1996)
[149] Anurag Singh (Translated & Edited), (1999:23) *Giani Kirapl Singh's Eye Witness Account of Operation Blue Star,* B. Chattar Singh Jiwan Singh, Amritsar
[150] Kushwant Singh was a famous commentator who wrote extensively for the press and authored many books. He recently died.
[151] Bhagat Puran Singh was a great humanitarian, he founded a hostel in Amritsar for people with disabilities, which has grown into an institution of welfare.
[152] Tridivesh Singh Malni in, Ahmed (2011: 73) *The Politics of Religion in South & South East Asia,* Taylor & Francis

This singular army action turned even moderates such as Giani Sant Singh Maskeen (1934 – 2005) – one of the highest regarded Sikh Scholars of the 20th century, to deliver speeches that would say we can no longer live in India and will now fight for our rights, with whatever means necessary, as our traditions teach us.[153] Sikhs soldiers mutinied in vain attempts to reach Amritsar, others went absent without leave, in total over 4000 did this.[154] These Sikh soldiers would all be later charged and many would be imprisoned for years to come. The government had underestimated the damage this action would cause and was unrepentant in its attitude afterwards; leading to more charged emotions.

This colossal event and its repercussions still live on with us today. The army and government officials are free to tell their side of the story, with the likes of General Brar consistently appearing in the media about the operation for the last 30 years. Whereas, eye-witnesses and defenders still are and have to be cautious, about where and with whom they share information about the operation – they have witnessed the liquidation of those that spoke the truth and witnessed their persecution (if they were not killed). This leaves a disjointed view of this historical event, but what is clear, is that the government and army tried in vain to whitewash the whole event, with a completely tainted and biased assessment of what occurred in the White Paper.

---

[153] A full discourse shortly after Operation Blue Star by Sant Singh Maskeen can be heard here
http://www.gurmatveechar.com/audios/Katha/02_Present_Day_Katha/Giani_Sant_Singh_Maskeen/Giani.Sant.Singh.Maskeen--1984.-.Response.to.Operation.Bluestar.mp3
[154] Kushwant Singh, (1991: 368), *A History of the Sikhs Vol. 2,* Oxford University Press, Delhi. See pages 33 – 36 of *Giani Kirapl Singh's Eye Witness Account of Operation Blue Star* - to find a detailed account. Also see pages 201 – 205 of Kirpal Dhillon (2006), Identity and Survival, Sikh Militancy in India 1978-1993. Penguin Books, Delhi.

It could be argued that the eye-witness reports are also biased, but the difference being, that these eye-witnesses risked everything in voicing what they viewed as the truth. Only those who were present in Operation Blue Star or Amritsar in June 1984 will know what really happened, and unfortunately with the passing of 30 years, many have now died.

General Brar recently appeared on the BBC Asian Network in the UK on a live debate on the 'Nihal Show'[155] – the discussion was centred on these specific events. He said, *"the objective was of clearing the temple (of the terrorists) who had fortified it and who were threatening to break away from the country. I mean, they had explosives, they had grenades, they had heavy weaponary. So the question wasn't anything else – but to clear the temple of the hostages."*

There are two points to address from his statement. Firstly, he maintains that there was a threat of a new nation being set up by these few hundred men inside the complex. We have already established that a separate state was not something Bhindranwale demanded, which immediately removes him and his men from this category. Yet it was Bhindranwale that the army were after. Also, how these Sikhs in Harmander Sahib would implement the setting up of a new nation was unclear – without commanding land and defending it, a new nation cannot be founded, this was not clearly occurring at this point.

The second point is that the main proponent of Khalistan in India, prior to the operation, was the General Secretary of the Council of Khalistan Balbir Singh Sandhu.

---

[155] On Wednesday 11th December, 2013. http://www.bbc.co.uk/programmes/p01n6qh0

He escaped from the complex on the night of the 5th June 1984 and took exile in Pakistan, until his death some years ago (as reported by the Tribune newspaper). So, in actual fact, the Operation did not achieve the objective of quelling secessionists as they were not present, or not killed. It actually gave birth to many more secessionists.

Later in the discussion, Brar agrees that innocent people would die as the army went in to capture the Gurdwara. Brar also alleges that the Sikh defenders held innocent people hostage – this is his accusation, and has not been verified by any independent research. The validity of his accusation raises questions over the absence of hostage demands by the Sikhs inside. Also, practically, one is made to question the likelihood of the defenders really choosing to fight the army on one hand, and holding pilgrims to hostage on another.

Nihal puts the following question to Brar at 20mins, *"....Violence on Harmander Sahib itself was extreme and completely disproportionate for the threat the Indian Army faced?"* Brar replied, *"Well that's the wrong opinion. The question is – we didn't expect the type of resistance offered ... certainly we did not want to use the tanks, the tanks were brought in as a last measure when we were approaching dawn – to knock out the top portions of the Akaal Takhat as they were holding out – they were killing soldiers. Our men were dying like flies ... Come daylight it would have become a major problem as thousands and thousands of Sikhs from the hinterland would have converged on the Golden Temple and it would have been a very sad day for the Indian army. So we had to complete the operation before then."* Here, Brar places the blame for the extreme use of force by the army on the defenders who were more prepared than the army. This was a shortcoming of the government who had been planning the attack for at least a year.

If the tanks had failed, an air strike would have had to be called. Brar admits the army was being slaughtered – giving credence to accounts of many more deaths of army personnel than suggested by the White Paper. Interestingly, his talk of Sikhs converging from the hinterland is spot on, as Sikhs could hear the bombardment of Harmander Sahib from up to 40 kilometres away. This caused Sikhs to start marches to Harmander Sahib, but many were killed by the army, as a curfew was in place, and shoot to kill orders were in action. Thus the reality of the repercussions of Operation Blue Star had already settled, the government and army were clearly aware, it would cause mass discord among the Sikhs. Rather than taking note of these consequences, the army forged ahead with causing more destruction to lives and the Gurdwara precincts.

Furthermore, Brar accuses the Sikhs at the Akaal Takhat of breaking Sikh traditions with the artillery that they used, *"... those are kirpans, you don't carry machine guns and rocket launchers. So those that were sitting at the Akaal Takhat were not armed in the typical Sikh way/tradition ... Indian army is apolitical."* Firstly, General Brar and anyone who questions the arms used by the defenders should go and make a closer study of Sikh History. They should go and view the guns of the Guru's stored in Gurdwaras across India.

Secondly, the word 'tupak' gun is used in Sikh Scriptures as mentioned earlier. About 1 kilometre away from Harmander Sahib is a Gurdwara called Lohgarh, at which there is a cannon used by the 6th Sikh Guru – so even the Guru's used explosives. Thus, guns and explosives have been part and parcel of the Sikh martial tradition from the times of the Gurus, and Sikhs, like any other martial race, will use the most modern arms available. Sikhs are not restricted to just use of the Kirpan as has been suggested by General Brar.

The point Brar makes about the apolitical nature of the army was clearly at odds with the army's own circular, Baatcheet (see Appendix 4), in which all practising Sikhs were declared as dangerous. The words in this article of Baatcheet would spur on the army to attack, arrest and torture Sikhs throughout Punjab, in the next army operation called Operation Woodrose.

Needless to say, the debates of what really went on, will continue, the readers can decide for themselves in what they believe.

Let us now briefly consider the other events of 1984, Operation Woodrose, Indira Gandhi's assassination and the anti-Sikh pogroms (massacres).

Operation Woodrose

Operation Woodrose was the next army operation after Blue Star, it would confirm the worst fears of most everyday Sikhs living in Punjab. The rhetoric of the White Paper and media euphoria of Sikh Terrorism would be escalated to the next level of discrimination, oppression and racism, against innocent Sikhs. The army was already deployed across Punjab due to Operation Blue Star, in the state-wide curfew that was imposed. Now, the army went into Sikh houses and arrested Sikhs. The Operation was a combing operation to sniff out any threats of revolt in the Sikhs.

"Village after village was surrounded, the houses of Sikhs (never Hindus) were searched for arms, Sikh young men taken for questioning, beaten up and tortured ... Amongst people charged and declared absconders and arrested were retired army officers."[156] Estimations of figures are very difficult to ascertain, due to the curfew in place, which lasted between 1 month to 3 months, depending on where people lived (districts near the border had a longer curfew).

8,000 people were reported as missing from their homes in October 1984,[157] the real death toll of civilians between June and July 1984, could be somewhere between 18,000 to 20,0000 – due to Operation Blue Star; deaths of civilians in marches to free Harmander Sahib; army attacks on other Gurdwaras; army mutineers; Operation Woodrose; and those who died in custody.[158]

Punjab became a state ruled by the army during this period. Due to the curfews in place, little evidence about the period is available, but what is evidently clear from all available accounts is that the army were very aggressive, violent and those arrested were commonly tortured. This brought on more misery for Sikhs in Punjab, as once an individual is arrested and has previous charges, he/she would always be a suspect in any future criminality in the locality that he/she resides in.

The security forces would then purposely harass these 'alleged' offenders in the future and bribing officialdom was the easiest and quickest way to gain

---

[156] Kuswant Singh (1991: 374), *A History of the Sikhs Vol. 2*, Oxford University Press, Delhi.
[157] Indian Express, 15 October, 1984
[158] Jaijee, (1999: 73) *Politics of Genocide*, Ajanta Publishing, Delhi

freedom. So, many of these 'alleged' offenders, took to arms to avoid this vicious cycle of arrest, torture and short-lived freedom outside of custody. They didn't necessarily do it out of revolutionary tendencies but a compulsion to survive.

What Bhindranwale, Dal Khalsa, Council of Khalistan and Babbar Khalsa could not achieve in 7 years, was achieved in a matter of one month by the actions of the Indian government and army. They created a secessionist movement, through their own actions, the anecdotal evidence and ideologies of Khalistani's now became a living reality and entered the ethos of the Sikh mind-set.

Indira Gandhi's assassination

On the 31st October 1984, Indira Gandhi was killed by two of her bodyguards - Beant Singh and Satwant Singh. Satwant Singh was hung in 1989, whilst Beant Singh died during interrogation in a clash with the security forces, shortly after the assassination. Much has been made of the fact that the assassins were Sikhs and were avenging the attack on Harmander Sahib. This fact was played on and used to further incite hatred and communal violence. This only increased the growing divisions between Sikhs and the Hindu majority of India.

However, when analysing this assassination, we must take one crucial factor into consideration, these bodyguards were employed to uphold the unity and dignity of the Indian Government. Their job was to protect the country and its integrity, through protection of its lead proponent the Prime Minister. In 1985, Leaf[159] argued that if the assassins felt that Indira Gandhi was actually causing

---

[159] Murray J. Leaf, *"The Punjab Crisis"* in Asian Survey, Vol.XXV, No.5, May 1985

the destruction of the country – they were morally compelled to protect India by doing what they did. Their act of violence can actually be viewed as an act of Indian nationalism in this context.

However, the media and higher authorities managed to manipulate the fact that they were Sikhs. It helped to project the opinion that Sikhs were the real enemies of India. This led to some of the most inhumane violence that India has ever witnessed. Her assassination helped project two things. Firstly, that no-one was safe from Sikhs. Secondly, that Sikhs were actually hell bent upon destroying India. This stoked further communal hatred, what was to follow her assassination, was inhumane and genocidal.

Anti-Sikh Pogroms

After Mrs Gandhi's assassination, violence was orchestrated against the Sikhs by the state and all the apparatus at its disposal. There is no denial of what occurred and all commentators of civil liberty both in India and across the globe have acknowledged that between 1st November – 3rd November 1984, Sikhs were openly torched alive, raped, displaced and made refugees in what they saw as their homeland (if they were lucky enough to survive). Gurdwaras that serve free food to the whole of humanity were not even spared, in Delhi alone, up to 200 Gurdwaras were attacked. Arson was the choice of destruction of the organised mobs.

The violence was a planned pogrom. Pogrom is a Russian word designating an organised and co-ordinated attack, accompanied by destruction, looting of property, murder, and rape, perpetrated by one section of the population against another. Or in simple terms, ethnic cleansing or genocide was enacted.

The Indian government has contended the notion that it was genocide and termed the events as anti-Sikh riots, however independent researchers have agreed that it was, *"... far from being a spontaneous expression of 'madness' and of popular 'grief and anger' at Mrs. Gandhi's assassination as made out to be by the authorities, were the outcome of a well-organised plan marked by acts of both deliberate commissions and omissions by important politicians of the Congress (I) at the top and by authorities in the administration."*[160] This quote is from an independent organisation that presented the truth of what went on, true to form their report was immediately banned in India; it can now be viewed online.[161] This report was published in February 1985 and is still banned today in India.[162]

More recently in a House of Lords debate in the UK on 3rd March 2014, Lord Indarjit Singh stated the following about these events, *"Orchestrated mobs went around Delhi and other major cities where the Congress (I) party of Indira Gandhi had influence and targeted Sikh homes, business and places of worship. Electoral registers were used and the police conveniently stood idle, Sikh officers were told to go home and Sikhs were disarmed by on duty officers, only to then be massacred.*

The widespread killing of thousands of Sikhs following Mrs Gandhi's assassination was blamed on spontaneous mob violence. All the evidence is that it was

---

[160] People's Union for Democratic Rights (PUDR) and People's Union for Civil Liberties (PUCL). *Who are the Guilty?* Delhi: Sunny Graphics, 1
[161] http://www.pucl.org/Topics/Religion-communalism/2003/who-are-guilty.htm
[162] 5 February 2014, Times of India

pre-planned for the anniversary of Guru Nanak's birthday and was simply brought forward, with the government-controlled All India Radio constantly inciting the killers with the words "Khoon ka badla khoon", meaning "Take blood for blood".

The army was confined to barracks for three full days to allow free rein to organised gangs carrying Sikh voter lists, armed with identical steel rods and an unusually plentiful supply of kerosene, to go around the capital in municipal buses beating and burning male Sikhs and gang-raping women and young girls. Prominent Hindus and Sikhs begged the new Prime Minister, Rajiv Gandhi, to order troops to restore order. His chilling response was: "When a big tree falls, the ground is bound to shake".

The same scenes were enacted throughout the country. We know all about the disappearances and killings in General Pinochet's Chile, but a WikiLeaks document carrying a signed report from the American embassy in India shows that more Sikhs were brutally murdered in just three days in 1984 than those killed in Pinochet's 17-year rule."[163]

After 30 long years – the Indian judiciary and government cannot clearly identify the guilty. Some convictions have taken place – but overall they are a mere drop in the ocean. The Indian Government declares that the casualties in Delhi numbered 2,733, but this seems very conservative, whilst other commentators and estimates

---

[163] http://www.theyworkforyou.com/lords/?id=2014-03-03a.1197.0&s=warsi

range from up to 10,000 in Delhi alone, and up to 20,000 throughout India.[164]

Many Sikhs lost their homes and businesses, the widowed lost their breadwinners; their husbands and sons. Sikhs became refugees in their own country and many fled to Punjab or areas of Sikh populations. Many never recovered and never will.

Hitler killed the Jews in gas chambers and hid the holocaust from the world. Sikhs were killed openly like aliens, in a nation that they viewed as their home, and at the time of these atrocities the world commonly referred to India, as 'the world's biggest democracy'.

Nation state heads lined up dutifully, for Indira Gandhi's state funeral and turned a blind eye to the massacre of Sikhs. The one life of Indira Gandhi was of more stature than the thousands of Sikhs killed, pillaged and raped. Successive governments have failed the Sikhs and continue to do so. When glaring atrocities cannot be acknowledged and justice delivered, through judicial means, what avenues do the Sikhs have left to seek justice? Many chose the path of vengeance and the gun – to fight and die with dignity, rather than die being tortured and murdered openly. These were the spurs of the Sikh secessionist movement, the cogs were in place and the lines were drawn. The war was to begin.

---

[164] To read more about the pogroms, please see also *"When a tree shook Delhi"* Manoj Mitta & H S Phoolka (2007) & *"Government Organised Carnage"* Gurcharan Singh Babbar (1998)

The Homeland

Sikh sentiments against the Indian state were at their pinnacle after 1984 and this led to the modern pursuit for Khalistan.[165] In 1986, the Sikhs convened a 'Sarbat Khalsa,' which is a gathering of the Sikh nation at the Akaal Takhat At this gathering on 26th January 1986 the Sikhs appointed a Panthic Committee[166] to lead the nation. A few months later they went on to make a declaration in pursuit of Khalistan on 29th April 1986 (see appendix 1 for the full declaration). In terms of the Sikhs "freely determining" their political status this was the Sikh nation's authentic expression of its wishes. Those Sikhs that then endeavoured to implement that national determination were systematically eliminated by India's armed forces in the years that followed.

I will now briefly give an overview of the concept of Khalistan and how it has emerged since the inceptions of the Sikh faith.

The Concept of Khalistan

What Khalistan constitutes is not a straight forward answer. Some say it's geographically bound to Punjab; others extend it to global domination.

Pro-Khalistanis point to the glorious past of Sikh Sovereign States and argue Khalistan should be based upon these. It is tied up with theology, geography, politics, and

---

[165] 'Khalistan' translates to the 'Land of the pure' – a Sikh Homeland
[166] Consisting of 5 Sikhs, Aroor Singh, Dhanna Singh, Gurdev Singh Usman Vala, Gurbachan Singh Manochahal & Vassan Singh Zafarwal. They appointed Gurdev Singh Kaunke as the Acting Jathedar (Leader), in the absence of Jasbir Singh Rode who was imprisoned at the time, but appointed Jathedar (Leader) of the Akaal Takhat nonetheless.

dare I say it – separatism! Some even refer to it as extremism and terrorism.

So where do we start? To gain some sort of clarity we need to review the argument through two lenses – those of a macro and micro nature. On a macro level, Khalistan in its simplest form is a vision to see a state ruled by Khalsa principles – the land of the Khalsa (the pure and those initiated into the Khalsa[167]). On a micro level Khalistan can mean something different for every individual and that's where the debates flare up. Is there any consistency? The simple answer is no.

Khalistan is viewed by some as the 'ideal' state – a dream far, far away. Others view it as a separatist threat that needs to be silenced.

Let us now turn to the historical and theological context of Khalistan or a 'Sikh homeland.' "Raj Karega Khalsa" is a common Sikh slogan that translates to 'The Khalsa will rule'. This slogan is quoted throughout the globe in Gurdwaras and homes, in the daily Ardas (supplication prayer) of a Sikh. Some argue the first Sikh Guru, Guru Nanak (1469 – 1539 AD), coined the term "Raj Karega Khalsa". Bhai Nand Lal (1633 – 1713 AD), a contemporary of the 10th Sikh Guru – Guru Gobind Singh (1666 – 1708 AD), mentions this term:

"The Khalsa will rule and the rebels will be eliminated. All will be obliged to join and only those who take sanctuary (in the Khalsa) will survive." (Tankahnama, Bhai Nand Lal)

---

[167] Those who become initiated as Sikhs become part of the Khalsa nation, they have to abide to its code of conduct

These are the exact lines that are quoted in the supplication prayer – originating from Bhai Nand Lal. Bhai Nand Lal's writing above is a conversation with himself and Guru Gobind Singh – so 'Raj Karega Khalsa' is stated by the Guru Himself.

Does 'Raj Karega Khalsa' really denote a geographical rule? Some would argue that the term in a micro sense refers to a victory of one's mind and unification with God. Therefore, this argument stems from a solely spiritual spectrum, hence here 'Raj Karega Khalsa' denotes purity in ruling your life when you become one with God. In which case, no rebels (vices) remain in you, as you have taken sanctuary in God. On a spiritual and more profound level, we can concede that this meaning can be accepted on a micro level and was favoured by the British during the Raj in order to quell independence movements. However, on a community/macro level, most Sikhs would argue it refers to a Sovereign nation of the Khalsa being founded.

Theologian's debate when this Khalistan will next be formed in a real geographical sense and the dates and length of this governance. These debates are based on contentious prophecies and as with any prophecies, the writings are vague and have general statements about how humanity will evolve and then the Khalsa Raaj (rule/Khalistan) will emerge. The debate about the length of the reign of Khalistan differs from 500 years, up to 5000 years.

Surprisingly, very few Sikhs know of these writings and perhaps these prophecies are the reason that debates occur on the authenticity of certain works. It is obvious that these prophecies would be seen as a threat to those who are in power, as they are the ones at risk of being debased[168]. Repression of knowledge is a key tool of propaganda wars, in order to 'control people' and follow 'political' agendas.

The modern fight for Khalistan

From 1984 to 1993, Sikhs waged a civil war of secession against India. Emotions were charged and many felt war was the only solution after the genocide of Sikhs in 1984. I purposely call it a war, in order to frame it within the frameworks of international law and theories on nationalism and statehood.

Mazzini (1871:153) described why war had to be undertaken against oppression. *"We disagree with those dreamers who preach peace at any cost, even that of dishonour, and who do not strive to make justice the sole basis of any lasting peace. We believe war to be sacred under certain circumstances. But war must always be fought within the limits of necessity, when there is no other way to achieve the good..."*[169] Furthermore, when discussing Mazzini's contributions to this topic, Recchia and Urbinati (2009) argue that, *"Where oppressive regimes and foreign occupation made any peaceful political contestation virtually impossible, violent insurrection would be legitimate and indeed desirable."*

The nationhood and history of Sikhs has been outlined in previous chapters. This denoted previous sovereign rule of the Sikhs and the way in which Sikhs make up a religious, ethnic, racial and national 'people.' The Sikhs

---

[168] Another source that talks of the emergence of Khalistan is the Sau Sakhi which is a collection of prophetic stories – said to authentically originate from the times of Guru Gobind Singh. Unfortunately it has been tampered with and many versions flood the market – thus authenticity is difficult to ascertain, but one thing is consistent and that is the mention of the creation of Khalistan.

[169] In Chapter Thirteen: Neither Pacifism nor Terror: Considerations on the Paris Commune and the French National Assembly (1871) 153

had exhausted the vestures of peaceful campaigns, after agitations since Indian independence, and the mass movement that was the peaceful Dharam Yudh Morch (civil disobedience campaigns between 1982 – 1984).

The Sikh Nation thus undertook a civil war in the hope of setting up a sovereign state in which they could enjoy freedom from oppression.

The Civil War

Having suffered two lethal and most humiliating blows to their sense of individuality and self-image, one after the other, at the hands of the Indian army during Blue Star and by Hindu mobs led by the ruling party leaders in November 1984, the Sikhs felt deeply mortified and could not look back into the past to construct a response in keeping with their historical experience to defend themselves against what they perceived as an oppressive and unjust state.
Kirpal Dhillon Ex-Director General of Punjab Police (2006:239)

In 1984, Sikhs were callously murdered and persecuted. Bhindranwale's words and speeches became prophetic, as what was anecdotal evidence of his speeches, now became a living reality of the Sikhs in India. This over-zealous discrimination of the Sikhs can be described as a declaration of war and an attempt to crush the Sikh Spirit once and for all.

The Sikhs in India had a year of endurance from 1984 – 1985, whereby many Sikhs were coming to terms with the harsh realities of modern India. They were viewed as criminals, anti-nationalists and treated as such, at every juncture. Even the Director General of the Punjab Police Kirpal Dhillon (July 1984 – September 1985) had to raise his pen and express his thoughts; describing his experience and analysis of these episodes in a very damming manner[170]. Dhillon talks of militancy in India in the following way, *"... India is especially vulnerable to eruption of major militant and insurgetnt movements and will continue to be so in the foreseeable future, given the proven ineptitude of its political and bureaucratic*

---

[170] Kirpal Dhillon, Identity & Survival, Sikh Militancy in India 1978 – 1993, Penguin Books India, 2006

leadership."[171] One must come to the conclusion that many wrongs were committed and the Sikhs had to fight to survive.

So what choice did Sikhs have, but to raise arms? They had seen that all the peaceful agitations of the Dharam Yudh Morcha culminated in the government responses of Operation Blue Star, Operation Woodrose and anti-Sikh pogroms. How could the youth of Punjab who were continually harassed, tortured and arrested, continue to live as second class citizens and treated like criminals? The excesses of the law by the security forces led to one inevitable conclusion – the drawing of the lines.

The Indian government had already declared war on the Sikhs through its actions in 1984. The Akaal Takhat was demolished; Harmander Sahib riddled with bullets; the Sikh Library was reduced to ashes and all artefacts looted. All the money boxes in the complex were looted as were ancient jewels and treasures. Sikhs were openly murdered and raped in the capital. Sikh youth were vilified, locked up, tortured and charged for crimes, without any evidence. The Sikhs took to arms and started a civil war for cessation, in defence of their nationhood and selves. The Sikh people, their history, their traditions and their physical presence was under attack. Militant groups arose and started to engage security forces in gun battles and assassinations. Revenge had begun and would continue until 1995.

Quelling the war

Julio Ribeiro was the Director General of Punjab Police between 1985 – 1989; he acknowledges that certain Sikh issues had to be addressed to mediate for peace. He

---

[171] P.xx in Kirpal Dhillon, Identity & Survival, Sikh Militancy in India 1978 – 1993, Penguin Books India, 2006

outlines them as two key points – the first being that those wrongly arrested in Operation Blue Star and subsequently detained in Jodhpur Jail had to be released, they were on the whole, normal innocent pilgrims and not 'terrorists.'[172] This was a reason for discord in normal people and a sign of continuing government oppression – he tried in vain to suggest the immediate release of the innocent prisoners, but instead, they were released intermittently which unduly delayed their incarceration.

The second point he thought needed addressing was the arrest and pursuit of the culprits of the anti-Sikh pogroms in Delhi 1984 – he raised this at many meetings and was advised to stop raising the point in the presence of Rajiv Gandhi[173]. In the end, when he did raise it again in Rajiv Gandhi's presence (who was then the Prime Minister), Gandhi lost his temper and told Ribeiro to stop making spurious claims for the pursuit of Sajjan Kumar and a legal process.[174] Sajjan Kumar has been one of the main accused instigators of the carnage since 1984 and is still making appearances in court cases to this effect. Rather than being punished, many like him and Jagdish Tytler were rewarded by the government for the heinous roles they played in the carnage; being promoted to seats in parliament and given portfolios as politicians.

No-one was exempt from prison. Twenty-two children and four women were held in Ludhiana jail after Operation Blue Star. The Supreme Court made an order for their immediate release which was not given effect to and when they were finally released, two of the children were re-arrested and sent to Nabha Jail.[175] New laws were

---

[172] Ribeiro, (1999: 302) *Bullet for Bullet. My life as a Police Officer*. Penguin Books India,
[173] The son of Indira Gandhi
[174] P.302, 304 ibid
[175] Amiya Rao et al, (1985: 7) *Oppression in Punjab,* Hind Mazdoor Kisan Panchayat Publication by Citizens for Democracy

passed to allow anyone to be held under suspicion of terrorism and only after paying hefty bribes were people freed from police custody. *"State terrorism has been unleashed on the Sikhs brandishing them as criminals ... sadistic torture of Amritdhari Sikhs and cold-blooded shooting down of young men in false encounters, are common occurrences, even village women are not spared ..."*[176] Vicious circles started, in which, people had to choose the gun, or flee from Punjab, or peacefully face harassment, arrest and torture. The worst hit areas were rural ones.

Sikh Insurgents

Let us briefly analyse the Sikh militants and their demands. By 1985, Sikh militant organisations such as the Khalistan Commando Force started to surface, the existing ones of Babbar Khalsa and the more politically based ones of Council of Khalistan and Dal Khalsa had already established a footing. The Damdami Taksal of Bhindranwale under the leadership of Baba Thakhur Singh (1915 – 2004) still had a massive grip on decision-making. The only other real major player was that of the Khalistan Liberation Force, although many splinter groups in the named existing organisations did emerge. The one singular figure who continuously had a major influence throughout the period was Dr Sohan Singh, who mysteriously reintegrated into the mainstream after this period. The All India Sikh Students Federation never really recovered after 1984 and was factionalised by many splinter groups, Daljit Singh Bittu became it's only leader of significance.

The Sikh militant organisations were fighting for independence from India (see appendix 2 declaration of Khalistan), but what they failed to do, was make

---

[176] Ibid P.9

progressive gains of land and defend them. So the nation-building of Khalistan had a rocky road, the Sikhs did gain small areas of control but they were never held on to, for too long. The Militant organisations did although initially also field support for candidates in elections and on the whole where their voice went, the candidates won. The Punjab is flat land and for insurgents to survive, they had to be housed in the homes of the general population and had to have grass-roots support in order to survive. So it was the people of Punjab who housed the militants.

Without gains in land and geographical victories – the battle was lost before it began. By 1989 many of the Sikhs in militant organisations started to lose heart and realised the harsh reality that their dream of Khalistan, was very far indeed. The militants would roam freely at night or engage in gun battles with the security forces if they were encountered and during the day they would mingle with the people. Ribeiro confirms this, *"It was commonly said in Punjab that the Police were in charge of the rural areas of the state during the daytime. At night, the terrorists took over since the police themselves were reluctant to step out at night."*[177] The militants didn't have the firepower, resources and might, to win the battle to victory. They would win in quick wins and would daringly fight and defeat the security forces in guerrilla tactics, but it was never more than that, sporadic victories.

The war that raged between the Sikhs and India, ran unabated largely between the years of 1984 – 1993. I say it ended in 1995 as the death of the Chief Minister Beant Singh hailed in a peaceful era. By the end of 1993, all the leaders of the numerous Sikh militant groups or dissidents,

---

[177] Ribeiro, (1999: 274) *Bullet for Bullet. My life as a Police Officer.* Penguin Books India,

had either been assassinated, imprisoned, or fled and took exile in Pakistan.

So who are the dead? Who were the casualties in this war? Regardless of sides; Sikh Militants or Punjab Police Officers; the important thing to note is that it was Punjabis that died. Punjab suffered as a state and in actuality the initial aims of the Indian government - to criminalise the Sikhs and repress the Punjab economically, socially and religiously, won out, and still render on.

Human Rights & Humans Wronged

Even though it was common knowledge that Ribeiro and KPS Gill (his predecessor)[178] were not the best of friends – they do agree on one thing, their dislike for human rights agencies. They both argue in their books that the human rights agencies were a front, for crying foul, when Sikh insurgents were either killed or arrested by the police. They argue these agencies did a great deal to break the morale of their officers and were an aide for the insurgents.[179] What both these Chiefs of Punjab Police tend to ignore, is the fact that they were employed as police officers to uphold the law, not unabashedly break it and cry, *"We are trying to save the nation at all costs."* A police officers job is to apprehend criminals not become a criminal.

Human rights agencies will always cry foul if atrocities are committed, as it is their remit to do so, but the police also have a moral, legal and legislative duty to stay within the law, when dealing with 'criminality' of any kind. Due to the police's extra-judicial practices – the

---

[178] They both held the Head of Police role in Punjab – Director General of Police between the majority of the civil war

[179] Ribeiro, (1999:306) *Bullet for Bullet. My life as a Police Officer.* Penguin Books India, and KPS Gill in *Knights of Falsehood*
http://www.satp.org/satporgtp/publication/nightsoffalsehood/

insurgents gained more support in Punjab, and the Punjab Police got international acclaim, for being one of the most brutal police forces in the world.

Ribeiro describes how he first recruited criminals to infiltrate the militant groups, but this back-fired as the criminals were just money-hungry and would just take orders from whoever paid the most, and engage in more criminality at will. After this failure, he set up infiltrator groups under the leadership of some of his police officers – the most notorious being Gobind Ram's and Azhar Alam's groups.[180] These police officers would attempt to infiltrate militant groups and kill with impunity, collecting huge bounties at the same time. They would also go around killing innocent people, whilst dressed as militants, in order to defame the militants and also commit heinous crimes on innocent villagers.

With the beginning of the reign of KPS Gill as the Director General of Police in 1989, the Punjab problem as it had become to be known, now started to become the Punjab killing grounds. KPS Gill with the green light from the centre, went all out to break the back of the movement. He did this by going outside the law and killing at will. When talking about the year 1988, KPS Gill says, *"What had been lacking was a clear mandate, and a freedom to carry on the battle without crippling political interference."* [181] What he means here, is that he wanted impunity to kill and quash the movement with any means necessary. He clarifies this point himself, *"... The message was, 'You confront us. Either we kill you or you kill us. Either you get arrested and lie in jail or you remain a*

---

[180] Julio Ribeiro, (1999: 348-350) *Bullet for Bullet. My life as a Police Officer.* Penguin Books India,
[181] KPS Gill, 1988, *Knights of Falsehood*
http://www.satp.org/satporgtp/publication/nightsoffalsehood/falsehood4.htm

fugitive. But there's a fourth way. You come, surrender to us and we assure you, you will undergo trial ... If 1800 policemen die, I tell you 5000 terrorists will die."[182]

KPS Gill's police force gained more combined terror when the Congress came to power in Punjab (February, 1992) and Beant Singh became the Chief Minister. The Sikh Militant groups signalled their own demise by boycotting the elections, Baba Thakhur Singh, Bhindranwale's successor had warned against the boycott as had Baba Gurbachan Singh Manochahal (the then leader of Khalistan Bhindranwale Tiger Force), but their words of advice fell on deaf ears. Dr Sohan Singh was in his ascendancy and had got Babbar Khalsa International, Khalistan Liberation Force and Khalistan Commando Force (led by Paramjit Singh Panjwar) under his wing, and with this alliance he led the campaign to boycott the elections. Between 1987 – 1992 Punjab had been under President's rule, so these were the first elections for a long time. There was a 24% turnout for the 1992 Punjab legislature election.[183] The Congress Party won the election and came to power in Punjab and Beant Singh became the Chief Minister.

With the Congress Party coming to power in Punjab – the Chief Minister Beant Singh, gave KPS Gill a clean chit to crush the movement, with any means necessary. So combing operations began, in which the Punjab Police would hunt and eliminate their most proclaimed offenders, for whom they had announced substantial bounties.

There was a typical process that was carried out. The

---

[182] Fernandes, (2006: 251) *A journey into the Heart of Indian Fundamentalism.* Portobello Books, London

[183] http://timesofindia.indiatimes.com/city/chandigarh/Punjab-breaks-records-records-77-voter-turnout/articleshow/11693925.cms

Punjab Police working with its network of informants would enter an area where a suspected militant had been. They would then go from home to home, killing people, until they started to speak and become informants. Thus killing sprees started.

Nobody was safe, even children of Congress politicians, normal Hindus, labourers from other states all came under attack. If by coincidence a suspected militant visited your locality, you would more than likely face the wrath of the police, unless you immediately started to give intelligence, which led to the death or arrest of the militant. Thus, through these methods – the militancy was eliminated.

Nowhere in this process were the hearts and minds of the Punjab populace won over, rather the rampant dislike and distrust of civil authorities and the Police in particular, continues to this day. People may have moved on, but they will definitely not forget what they have had to endure; the terror by an authority they were meant to trust. Even if we were to believe that the aim of the government to remove terrorism was in the interests of the people; their tactics certainly did not show it. There was no winning over hearts and minds – just clinical expulsion.

Proving unlawful killings, led to the death of Jaswant Singh Khalra, a human rights activist. Khalra had uncovered mass cremations of unidentified bodies, leading him to start a campaign to get justice for the dead. These unidentified bodies were of those Punjabi people who had been killed en masse by the police, and then callously disposed of; the law requires for the bodies of unidentified people to be investigated. Some records existed of the cremations and authorisations existed for unidentified bodies to be cremated, but no records of attempts to identify the dead were in place – making these cremations illegal.

The law was flaunted and now armed with this evidence, Khalra had a clear case of malfeasance of those police officers who had ordered the cremations. In the end, Khalra was threatened and told he would become another statistic of the dead, and true to form, the Punjab Police delivered its promise and he did die at the hands of the Police on 6th September 1995 (he had only made the discovery in January 1995). Eventually, in 2005, five Punjab Police officers were convicted of his murder.

Legal challenges were launched to investigate these mass cremations of unidentified bodies, leading to the Supreme Court acknowledging flagrant violations of human rights on a mass scale in its order on 12 December 1996.[184] Khalra had uncovered 2097 illegal cremations had taken place, with 1238 of the deceased being classed as unidentified, and 247 as partially identified, spanning three cremation grounds in Amritsar.

Some of the families have been compensated, 1097 families of those illegally cremated have received compensation, but the judicial process has failed in a number of ways. No police officers have been investigated or arrested for the illegal detention and deaths of those identified. The police and state have successfully controlled the process, ensuring no other cremation grounds were investigated. The loved one's of those that just 'disappeared,' live on in doubt, of what really happened to their family members, no closure is in sight.

Pursuit of perpetrators of the war

---

[184] Kumar, (2008: 6) *Terror in Punjab*, Shipra Publications, Delhi,

So, today, those Punjab Police Officers that murdered in the name of Indian nationalism are being pursued by Human Rights activists and seekers of justice. They are pursued in India and Sikhs for Justice[185] are successfully lodging cases to block entry and pursue those in office, in the USA through its judicial system. These officers and the Indian army personnel who committed excesses, are also branded 'war criminals' by Sikhs all over the globe and hotly pursued.

Similarly, Sikhs who waged war against the Indian state are either imprisoned in India, living in exile in foreign countries or banned from entry into India. So, these Sikhs still also feel the repercussions of this war. Those jailed in India are in a pitiable state and many have served life sentences with no freedom in sight. Those who did engage in militancy and didn't abuse their power of the gun, have mostly fell into economic disarray and are ruined due to their sacrifices for the movement.

In short, both parties of the war – who are Punjabi still suffer (insurgents and the Punjab Police). Those in power in Delhi (the Central Government), never really suffered and never will. The centre just recharged Punjab with national debt of these years of militancy, which Punjab has had to repay; only adding to the social, political and economic problems of Punjab.

What should have followed this civil war, under international conventions of war, is that prisoners of war are returned and a peace deal struck to end hostilities. Much like the Good Friday Agreement, in the Northern Ireland dispute, which hailed in peace, through a mutual agreement, to move forward without acts of violence.

---

[185] A US Based advocacy group http://www.sikhsforjustice.org/?q=contact_us

The prisoners of war in the case of this civil war would be Sikhs imprisoned for committing crimes in their fight for self-determination. Now, this was never done, as if it had been done the Indian government, would have had to accept that a war took place under international conventions.

The Indian government and all the commentators aligned with its nationalistic viewpoint choose to view the conflict mostly as a law and order problem; proclaiming only a minority of Sikhs fought for Khalistan. Kirpal Dhillon agrees on this restrictive definition of the conflict, *"Sikh militancy in Punjab continued to be treated as a mere law and order problem even though it showed all the characteristics of a political movement."*[186] Agreeing to a war like situation would have meant having to take a mature and sensible outlook, to resolve some of the insipient issues that led to the war taking place. Therefore, a freeing of Sikh political prisoners and an acceptance by Punjab Police or Indian Security Forces, that they also worked outside the law during this war. An agreement to this effect; accepting the wrongs of both sides in stepping outside of the law, would have had to be accepted, and agreements to reign in peace.

Thus, a non pursuit of the Punjab Police would also have to be accepted by Sikhs and their organisations. A drawing of a line, agreeing to wrongs done on both sides and a moving on, to ensure such issues do not arise in the future. India chose to instead view it as a mere, law and order problem, ignoring the political nature of the movement. Political conflicts can always be revived, unless they are dealt with through mutual dialogue.

---

[186] Dhillon, (2006: xix) *Identity & Survival, Sikh Militancy in India 1978 – 1993*, Penguin Books India,

If we reflect for one moment – with what happened with the Jews and the Nazi's. Many similarities can be drawn with the Sikh cause or Punjab problem. The facts are non-deniable of what went on, with both the Sikhs and the Jews. The Jews successfully gained positions of power in Western governments and then went about establishing Israel. The conflict in Israel still rages in some proportions, but they have reclaimed Israel. The Sikhs who lived through the period of militancy in Punjab, had to flee from Punjab, to survive, and they today, now lead this movement for self-determination (mostly in Western countries). It is small in proportions but it continues nonetheless.

The Post-War Period
1994 - 2014

To reflect upon the last 20 years, we must first contextualise the whole era of the last 30 years, and the interaction between Sikhs and the Indian state. Living as a Sikh in the Diaspora, like many others, I have had interactions with those opposed to the official Indian Governmental line of this recent history. Reflecting on this period and through my academic studies, has led me to the conclusion that this period and its continuation into today, can only be termed 'the politics of genocide.' I will now analytically present how I came to this conclusion and the harsh realities, are, indeed, disturbing.

Politics of Genocide

Genocide is defined as *"any of the following acts committed with intent to destroy, in whole or in part, a national, ethnical, racial or religious group ... as the deliberate killing of a large group of people, especially those of a particular nation or ethnic group."* This is the definition as agreed by the 1948 United Nations Convention on the Prevention and Punishment of the Crime of Genocide Article 2.

Genocide Watch outlines 8 stages of genocide, namely:

1. Classification
2. Symbolisation
3. Dehumanization
4. Organization
5. Polarization
6. Preparation
7. Extermination

8. Denial[187]

The first stage of genocide is classification. It was enacted by classifying the Sikhs and creating a divide of "us" & "them." The Sikhs are a religious and racial group, religiously distinct from other faiths and racially distinct, as through their practice of faith, their external articles of faith make them racially recognisable. So the wearing of turbans, Kirpans, unshorn hair and flowing beards, makes the Sikhs racially distinct. Sikhs have thus vehemently contested Article 25 of the Indian constitution, which classifies them as Hindus. Due to their minority status, and the denial of Punjabi in Punjab, made them feel threatened even more. The Sikhs, then started peaceful campaigns, to realise these rights, which made it even easier to make the classification of those 'rebellious Sikhs' and 'us' the mainstream peaceful community and so forth.

Symbolization was achieved by combining hatred, with symbols associated with the Sikhs. So the Indian Army circular (see appendix 4) labelled all practicing Sikhs (Amritdharis) as criminals. The colour orange was labelled as a symbol of terrorism and Sikhs were labelled secessionists and separatists, long before 1984. This was done in an attempt to malign all Sikhs. The colour orange is the national colour of the Sikhs – the Sikh national flag (Nishan Sahib) is usually of this colour. 'Sikhs' were thus viewed as being synonymous with trouble, as portrayed by the Indian Government and its media. Other points pertaining to this symbolization, have been covered in previous chapters.

However, one may argue that the President of India in 1984 (Giani Zail Singh), was a Sikh and Sikhs also held

---

[187]http://www.genocidewatch.org/aboutgenocide/8stagesofgenocide.html

other prolific positions in governance and society. That was the case, but these Sikhs in these positions, largely failed their role as Sikhs, by not voicing their opinions and turning a blind eye to the human rights abuses taking place. For example, Giani Zail Singh admitted in his memoirs that he was not fully aware of the attack upon Harmander Sahib and that he felt helpless when Sikhs were being massacred across India, after Indira Gandhi's assassination.[188]

He termed the violence after Indira Gandhi's assassination, a holocaust, in his memoirs. As the President of India he was the head of state and armed forces, yet he didn't wield the power that his seat held and rather chose to be obedient and not challenge his political colleagues. Other Sikhs chose to fight the system from within and many more quit their posts.

Dehumanizing the Sikh community, took place through acts of state persecution – such as not allowing Sikhs entry into Delhi for the Asian Games in November 1982. It has to be acknowledged that the Akali's had threatened to peacefully protest at the games, but surely that did not criminalise the whole Sikh population? Road blocks and cordons were set up and Sikhs were singled out to be barred from entry into Delhi, sending a clear signal of discrimination against all Sikhs. Bhindranwale had said that, *"... the press is terming the 'Sikhs' as extremists, yet the constitution says we are Hindus – so does that make us Hindu extremists?"* He argued, either the Sikhs were accepted as a distinct faith, or they should be maligned as right wing Hindus, if the term extremism is to be used. A moral panic was created, that some Sikhs are hell bent on destroying the unity of India, thus dealing with these

---

[188] Memories of Giani Zail Singh, The Seventh President of India. 1997

enemies of the state, by any means became acceptable, as they were viewed as sub-human.

The stages of organisation and polarization were enacted by the use of the security forces through killing squads. Sikhs were killed in Operation Blue Star, Operation Woodrose and the anti-Sikh pogroms. They were then pursued throughout Punjab by fake militant groups (at the behest of the state), black cats (police commandos) and turncoats and infiltrators, who worked with the government.

The Punjab was polarized. Sikhs fled to other areas of the country and took refuge from areas where anti-Sikh pogroms had been committed. Thus the Sikhs could easily be targeted in Sikh ghettos or neighbourhoods. After the partition of 1947, some Sikhs were re-housed in specific colonies of Delhi – these would later be the ones targeted by the anti-Sikh pogroms. Be it by fate or design, this became a reality of modern India. The other stages of preparation and extermination became party to these designs.

The last and final stage of genocide is its denial. This is the scariest element of genocide, as its denial means that acts of genocide can be re-enacted, as the offending community/nation has no acceptance of the crimes committed. The continual denial of the Indian government and its representatives, of mass murder of Sikhs in Operation Blue Star, Operation Woodrose and anti-Sikh pogroms continues unabated. The Sikhs and Hindus of Punjab, were then killed by the Punjab Police in trying to contain the separatist movement of Khalistan whilst this was accepted to an extent, denial begins when it gets to judicial reviews and the pursuit of the officers. So by and large the Sikhs are told to accept the atrocities, murders and, quite simply, the state terrorism.

Between 1984 and 1993, the Sikhs waged a civil war against the state, one could argue that the whole Sikh community didn't wage war and it was a minority, but tacit support and agreement with the actions of separatists can mean support and engagement in this war. If one were to look at real armies and conflicts across the globe – the army is only a small percentage of the nation state that it represents.

Similarly, those that took to arms and/or politically espoused self-determination, didn't necessarily have to be outwardly a majority to represent their nationality. Also, openly supporting and engaging in the war, would usually lead to death, persecution and pursuit by the state apparatus, so it would be smart of the majority of people to not openly engage in activities and tacitly support them.

1995 - 2014

This period represents peace in Punjab. Although it must be acknowledged that the party politics and policies of successive governments were geared to achieve specific motives – those of subduing Sikhs, and any sort of revolutionary tendencies; thus in effect controlling dissent and ensuring no revival of militancy. Now, that may seem acceptable and the normal path to undertake for some, but when this path actually leads to the destruction of socio-economic factors for the people of Punjab, it can become the policy that bites back and delivers the militancy, that you are actually trying to subdue.

KPS Gill mirrors these thoughts of unaddressed latent issues that led to the insurgency. In 2004 he had the following to say, *"... I was often asked whether terrorism could ever return to the state, and my answer, invariably, was confidently in the negative ... Today I am not as certain of this as I was some years ago. Punjab had, for the past decade, been outrageously governed, with incompetence and rampant corruption ... Sikh farmers and at least some among these proud people have been driven to suicide by debt and a deteriorating rural economy ... the continuing failure to meet even minimal aspirations of the young and underprivileged, now make it difficult to entirely exclude the possibility of a revival of the politics of extremism and violence ..."*[189]

The Punjab now has a horrendous list of growing socio-economic problems that need to be tackled to avoid future problems for the Punjab. I will now detail each of the socio-economic problems that the Punjab now faces.

Education

The level of education acts as a good indication of the standards of living and the future prospects of a region. The literacy rates collected from the 2011 census show that Punjab is positioned 19th out of the 35 states in India. Its literacy rate stands at 76.7%; with the highest being 93.9% in Kerala.[190]

Punjab is, and has been, one of the most economically vibrant states of India since the 1970's, so a progressive outlook in nurturing this economic stature would be expected in terms of expenditure on education. To the contrary, state expenditure on education in Punjab dropped from 22.17% in 1970 to a mere 12.33% in 2008.[191]

---

[189] KPS Gill (2013: x), in "The Punjab Story" Amarjit Kaur et al, Roli Book
[190] http://www.mapsofindia.com/census2011/literacy-rate.html
[191] Project No Village Left Behind Punjab, Booklet by The Kalgidhar Trust – Baru Sahib,

The Punjab population resides mainly in rural areas with 66% living in rural areas and rural literacy is at 65% whereas urban literacy is 79%. This rural disparity is more profound when studying enrolments at university with only 2,085 rural students out of 56,240 enrolled on professional courses in Punjabi universities.[192]

In Punjab, education is a booming industry with private schools and English medium schools being very popular. The state schools are seen as poor by the population and private tutoring is popular, as are private educational institutes, but unfortunately regulation of education is poor and private institutes charge high fees and the results are not representative of the funds invested.

Also, job prospects in Punjab are very poor, hence further and higher education are not viewed as beneficial by the general public, due to the lack of opportunities, this is especially so, for those from rural areas.

Alcohol abuse

Punjab is known as the land of five rivers, nowadays Alcohol is commonly referred to as the sixth river, it flows freely throughout the state with little restriction and is a cash cow of the Punjab state government, through taxation and revenues. *"There are eight thousand liquor stores in the state. A large share of the state revenue is obtained by the auction of these stores and taxes on the sale of liquor. According to official figures, the Punjab state realized about 2374 crore (billion) rupees as excise duty in 2010-11 and consumption of liquor was about 11 litres per month per person."* [193]

---

[192] "Professional Education in Punjab: Exclusion of Rural Students" Ranjit Singh Ghuman et al, Punjabi University, Patiala – the report can be viewed at http://www.fao.org/fileadmin/templates/ERP/uni/PEPJ.pdf
[193] http://sikhinstitute.org/july_2012/12-sawan.html 1 crore = 10 million

If we compare alcohol consumption with the national average of 26%, the residents of Punjab have 49.8% alcohol intake[194], almost double the national average. Records show that liquor consumption increased by 29% between 2005 and 2010, and that, *"During election days bottles and synthetic drugs rule the society as voters are lured by the candidates who secretly distribute them free."*[195]

Alcohol abuse though is not just confined to Punjab; Punjabis all over the globe have built up a reputation for being heavy drinkers and throwing the most lavish parties, where alcohol flows freely. So the onus is on all Punjabis to address this rampant social evil from their lives and culture. It has no place in the Sikh faith, but most westerners are shocked when they learn of this tenant of the faith, as most Sikhs that they have come across are non-practising and drink heavily.

Drug Abuse

Punjab has the highest intake of opium, opioid and heroine in the whole of India, as reported by the Ministry of Social Justice & Empowerment and the United Nations International Drug Control Programme.[196] A study conducted by the Ministry of Youth Affairs and Sports in 2011, noted that, *"40% of Punjabi youth in the age group of 15 to 25 years have fallen prey to drugs."*[197]

There is also widespread agreement that local politicians and police take a cut of the drug profits. Election officials seized more than 100 pounds of heroin

---

[194] http://www.nyks.org/hindi/Drug%20Abuse%20Punjab%20Eng.pdf
[195] http://sikhinstitute.org/july_2012/12-sawan.html
[196] http://www.nyks.org/hindi/Drug%20Abuse%20Punjab%20Eng.pdf
[197] Advani, Rahul, "Factors Driving Drug Abuse in India's Punjab", ISAS Working Paper, no 177-24, Spetmeber 2013.

that they said party workers intended to distribute to voters before state elections in January 2012. Giving out alcohol to bribe potential constituents is relatively common in India, but the plan to distribute heroin was unique to Punjab.[198]

What reforms do the Punjab people expect from politicians who get elected via bribing the masses through free alcohol and drugs? This is one of the lowest ebbs of politics in India and Punjab has taken it to a new level, in terms of illicit drugs distribution as well.

The Punjab Police usually put drugs back into the market, *"If they confiscate 100 packets, police show 50 to the press and let the other 50 back into the market."*[199] There have been high-profile cases across India and Punjab of drug smugglers and dealers, working with corrupt officials and politicians.

Punjab has the highest rate of drug seizures, *"roughly 60 per cent of all illicit drugs confiscated in India are seized in Punjab"*[200] This portrays the gravity of the problem, as this is the detection rate, meaning that the actual levels of drugs entering Punjab is much higher. Punjab is a border state and smuggling does take place across the border, but other border states such as Gujrat and Rajasthan don't experience the same levels of drug detection or abuse.

Each Punjabi family has been affected by drug abuse, everyone knows someone who has had a drug problem, as it is so rampant. *"The vibrant Punjab that had*

---

[198] http://www.washingtonpost.com/world/drug-epidemic-grips-indias-punjab-state/2012/12/31/092719a2-48f6-11e2-b6f0-e851e741d196_story.html
[199] http://www.washingtonpost.com/world/drug-epidemic-grips-indias-punjab-state/2012/12/31/092719a2-48f6-11e2-b6f0-e851e741d196_story.html
[200] http://www.nyks.org/hindi/Drug%20Abuse%20Punjab%20Eng.pdf

ushered in the green revolution is today living in a dazed stupor as 67 per cent of its rural households has at least one drug addict."[201]

Most drug addicts are between the ages of 16 to 35 years old. Dr. P. D. Garg, a psychiatrist at the state-run Guru Nanak Dev Hospital said, *"If we don't do anything about this problem, one entire generation of youth will be wiped away. There is no political will and the awareness campaigns need to be stepped up."*[202]

The drug and alcohol problem isn't one of peasantry only, it cuts across all spheres of the social structure and the the wealthy[203] also indulge in these habits. It has become engrained into the youth culture of Punjab - where 7 out of 10 college-going students suffer from drug abuse.[204] A survey by Guru Nanak University in Amritsar *"suggested that as much as 70% of young Punjabi men were hooked on drugs or alcohol."*[205] Furthermore, *"In Punjab the numbers are ridiculous - nearly 75% of its youth are severely addicted to drugs, that's 3 out of every 4 children."*[206]

Economics – Fiscal performance

The green revolution in Punjab made Punjab boom as an economy and it produced a large return of cash remittances, estimated to be the second largest of any state after Kerala.[207] This is the dichotomy of Punjab – wealth

---

[201] http://archive.indianexpress.com/news/every-third-male-student-in-punjab-drug-addict-hc-told/464048/
[202] http://www.dw.de/drug-abuse-threatens-punjabs-population/a-16683761
[203] http://www.bbc.co.uk/news/world-south-asia-11925617
[204] http://archive.indianexpress.com/news/every-third-male-student-in-punjab-drug-addict-hc-told/464048/
[205] http://www.bbc.co.uk/news/world-south-asia-11925617
[206] http://deaddictioncentres.in/news/indias-youth-drugs/
[207] http://www.financialexpress.com/news/why-punjab-has-suffered-long-steady-decline/1028411

and affluence as a state, but this is now stagnating, and the once prosperous and hard-working Punjabis can no longer meet their ambitions and aspirations, leading to substance misuse and a raft of other social problems. Even though the Punjab economy boomed early on, it is now stagnating, between 2002-11, Punjab's GDP growth was lower than the national average at only 6.61% in comparison to 7.95%.[208]

One of the many myths about Punjab's financial decline is that the Sikh Separatist movement led to this decline. The separatist movement ended two decades ago, and Punjab's decline has continued nevertheless. *"To regain its place in the sun, Punjab's politicians need to abandon old myths about why it is in trouble and face up to some ugly realities. The state needs to tackle its chronic fiscal deficit, something that holds back investment in education, health and infrastructure, and focuses public spending on various unproductive subsidies, the most fiscally crippling of which is free power for farmers, mainly for electricity."*

The free electricity may be crippling the state, but it is a short term solution and a vote winning ploy. The farmers need free electricity to make their farming viable and profitable, as the government fixed prices for their crops make them very little profits and diversification is only attempted by the brave or established farmers, as it is a venture into the unknown for many. The state needs to support the farmers and work on viable solutions with the support of the centre – as the current system is not sustainable and is flawed.

---

[208] http://www.financialexpress.com/news/why-punjab-has-suffered-long-steady-decline/1028411

Many farmers are now riddled with debt with 85% of Punjab's farmers reeling under a heavy debt burden.[209] Farmers end up borrowing money from loan sharks at exorbitant interest rates and repayment conditions.[210] This is due to the paucity of funds to support them, so they have no choice but to fight for their survival in more precarious loan schemes, in which they usually get in more debt, rather than ride out their difficulties. Punjab Agricultural University estimates that farmer debt has risen to Rs 35,000 crore (3.5 billion Rupees). [211]

The most recent figures we could source, from 2013 suggest that, *"According to Economic Survey of the state, contribution of primary sector (which comprises mainly agriculture and allied activities) in the GDP of state is continuously declining since 2004-05 when it was 32.67% and it is likely to come down to 21.83% in 2012-13 (advance estimates) ... As per latest definition of Poverty , 15.9 % of population was still living below Poverty line in Punjab. Although this poverty ratio of Punjab was nearly half of National level (29.8 %)."[212]* For a state that was once the tiger economy of India, to have even 15% of the population living in poverty, is shocking.

The state has been pillaged for its water, crops and Punjabis haven't had the long-term strategic thought that was required to carry its previous economic performance forward. Decrepit dynasties ravage the political scene and whilst Punjab has developed serious socio-economic problems allied to its early economic performance, other

---

[209] http://www.dayandnightnews.com/2012/03/punjab-farmers-reeling-under-heavy-debt-burden/
[210] http://saanjh.org/programs/adopt-a-family
[211] http://www.dayandnightnews.com/2012/03/punjab-farmers-reeling-under-heavy-debt-burden/
[212] http://www.business-standard.com/article/economy-policy/punjab-facing-stagnancy-in-agriculture-state-s-economic-survey-113033000131_1.html

states throughout India have developed at an alarmingly faster rate.

Punjab is no longer the labourer's promised land, and Punjab will soon no longer be the granary of India, as reliance on Punjab is decreasing as investments in other states have led to their agricultural and economic advances. With increasing trade across borders with Pakistan and an increasing global economy, Punjab needs to compete in trade in more efficient ways.

Water

The Punjab is suffering with a water crisis, both in terms of its supply and cleanliness. Most of Punjab's water for agriculture is sourced from the ground, but over usage of these reserves has led to multiple issues, with 85% of the state suffering from declining levels, that is an approximate decrease of 60cm each year and nitrate levels have gone up tenfold in the last four decades.

A member of the legislative assembly (MLA) Kler summarises the water crisis that Punjab is facing, *"This means that water in Punjab will cease to be potable for humans and animals in the next 20-25 years."* Over use and high levels of pesticides and pollutants used for agriculture, have led to this crisis, in which ground level water reserves of the last 105 years have been used up.[213] Added to this, water from the ground is pumped through tube wells, these tube wells rely on electricity to pump the water – thus another resource dependency of electrical power comes into the play. Up to 70% of the cultivatable land in Punjab is irrigated through these tube wells.[214]

---

[213] http://timesofindia.indiatimes.com/india/Ground-water-level-declining-contamination-rising-in-Punjab/articleshow/14482758.cms?referral=PM
[214] http://archive.indianexpress.com/news/ in-punjab-groundwater-level-recedes-by-33-cm-daily-due-to-waterintensive-agri-/1167008/

Punjab is one of the states appointed to contribute to the central government reserves of rice. Rice cultivation is water intensive and traditionally relies on seasonal rainfall. Rice cultivation is one of the main income generators for Punjabi farmers, but its water usage is excessive, *"For producing one kilogram of rice, Punjab consumes 5,400 litres of water, whereas West Bengal consumes only 2,400 litres. This water-intensive cultivation process is causing groundwater levels in Punjab to recede by 33 cm every day."*[215] The reality is that Punjab is in danger of becoming a desert within the next 20 years, if the water crisis is not addressed and/or diversification of agriculture doesn't occur.

Replenishment of ground water is required, as is better management of existing water and conservation of water supplies. *"From 1982-87, the water table in Central Punjab was falling an average of 18 cm per year. That rate of decline accelerated to 42 cm per year from 1997-2002, and to a staggering 75 cm during 2002-06. Water tables are now falling over about 90 percent of the state, with Central Punjab most severely affected. The potential effects of groundwater depletion include the drying up of wells, reduced stream flows, deteriorating water quality and sinking land, as well as increased costs and lower profit margins for farmers. In Punjab, smaller farmers are the first to suffer; as production costs rise, many are forced to take on debts they cannot hope to repay. As a result, the once prosperous farmers of Punjab suffer."*[216] Punjab has a good canal system, which helps irrigate agriculture but only 27 per cent of the state is irrigated with canal water.

---

[215] http://archive.indianexpress.com/news/-in-punjab-groundwater-level-recedes-by-33-cm-daily-due-to-waterintensive-agri-/1167008/
[216] http://water.columbia.edu/research-projects/india/punjab-india/

The remaining 73 per cent area is irrigated through groundwater pumped out through tubewells.[217]

The current day Indian Punjab has the rivers Sutlej, Beas and Ravi flowing through it. River waters and their sharing is a very politicised issue and many states are reliant on river waters for farming and generating electricity. Punjabis have campaigned for the rights of their rivers and the current Chief Minister of Punjab, Parkash Singh Badal, said in 2010, *"Like minerals, river water is an asset of Punjab and any use of it by other states should be accounted for in terms of money,"*[218] This statement may be seen as partisan, in terms of only looking at Punjab's interests, but many Punjabis see an injustice done to their state, when they have to suffer power cuts and incur extra living costs for clean water and so forth.

More interestingly, it was the Congress Party Chief Minister, Captain Amarinder Singh back in 2004, who put the Sutlej Yamuna Link canal[219] construction to a permanent halt – through the enactment of the Punjab Termination of Agreements Act which terminated the obligations of Ravi-Beas water sharing with Haryana. The construction of the canal would lead to a definite loss of waters from Punjab and has been a point of contention for the last 40 years. The conflict about this water sharing is now at the Supreme Court since 2004 – with no outcome in sight, as of yet.[220]

---

[217] http://www.dayandnightnews.com/2012/03/punjab-farmers-reeling-under-heavy-debt-burden/
[218] http://www.dnaindia.com/india/report-punjab-and-haryana-spar-over-river-water-royalty-1400088
[219] Whenever this canal has been attempted to be constructed in Punjab, the workers constructing it, have been killed. Its construction is a very volatile issue and damning the river water would mean economic demise of the Punjabi farmers who rely on the river water that would be diverted.
[220] http://www.archive.india.gov.in/sectors/water_resources/index.php?id=14

Farming

In the 1970's, the Indian government set out plans to combat famine and poverty. This encompassed the green revolution in Punjab, whereby the state of Punjab became India's granary, abolishing dependency on food aid.[221] Punjab led the revolution of combating the nation's poverty through its agricultural renaissance. Whilst the whole of India, including Punjab, benefitted from this, the long term ecological and social effects were not considered.[222]

Punjab only makes up 1.5 per cent of India's geographical span and produces 70% of the nation's wheat and contributes to the central pools of wheat and rice by contributing 40% of its rice and between 55-60% of its wheat.[223] Ironically, the frequent problem of the farmers is of production glut.[224] So the farmers of Punjab actually over-produce, leading to lower prices for their crops and being paid by private agents to get any cash to shift their harvests when desperation sets in.

More recent figures show less dependence on Punjab for its crops, during 2011-12, 38.7% wheat and 22.1% rice to the central pool was contributed by the state. *"The Agriculture production in the state has reached a plateau. The soil health in the state has been deteriorating with the continuation of rice-wheat rotation by farmers due to assured profits as compared to other crops."*[225]

Farmer Suicides

---

[221] http://www.financialexpress.com/news/why-punjab-has-suffered-long-steady-decline/1028411
[222] http://water.columbia.edu/research-projects/india/punjab-india/
[223] http://www.dayandnightnews.com/2012/03/punjab-farmers-reeling-under-heavy-debt-burden/
[224] http://www.dayandnightnews.com/2012/03/punjab-farmers-reeling-under-heavy-debt-burden/
[225] http://www.business-standard.com/article/economy-policy/punjab-facing-stagnancy-in-agriculture-state-s-economic-survey-113033000131_1.html

Between 2000 and 2011, *"... a total 6,926 farmers and labourers had committed suicide in the state, of which 3,954 were farmers and 2,972 labourers. It also revealed that 75% farmers committed suicide due to debt while 29% labourers ended their lives for the same reason."*[226] For this period, this aggregates to at least 52 suicides a month. As the data was not complete, a fresh study is under way, which started in 2013, it will attempt to aggregate all the data Punjab-wide and make a comprehensive assessment of suicides. This study has been commissioned by the Punjab Government.

The last two decades

The above is a glimpse of the facts, of what is occurring in the socio-economic spheres in Punjab, it does not make inspiring reading. The research that was conducted to collate this data was very limited in its scope and has only looked at some of the headline issues. Other spheres such as health and well-being have been completely omitted and up to date data on some of the issues was not obtained. Punjab is still although a highly successful state in terms of its economic performance.

When one visits Punjab, one will see exuberant shopping malls and a world torn between modernity and a rural village lifestyle. Smart phones are widely owned and those that live in Punjab have high aspirations and wish to excel economically and live the dream, of being affluent. Unfortunately, many are now being crushed in the pursuit of this dream and as expectations are not met; other social evils enter their lifestyles to escape their feelings of under-achievement.

---

[226] http://timesofindia.indiatimes.com/city/chandigarh/Punjab-plans-fresh-survey-on-farmer-suicides/articleshow/21907305.cms

The last 30 years can be viewed in the following way. For a decade (1984-1994) a civil war was waged between the Sikhs and the Indian Government. Both sides engaged in killings, you knew who your enemy was to a certain extent.

However, over the last two decades (1994 – 2014), be it by design or default, the Punjabi people have been pillaged by socio-economic factors leading to their decline or degeneration. A loss of faith has parried this, now in some villages in Punjab you won't find a single young boy who keeps his hair unshorn (especially so in Nawanshaer and Jalandhar districts).

The revolutionary spirit of Sikhs cannot awaken, as the Sikhs themselves, are too busy dealing with their day to day lifestyle issues of putting food on the table. Also, poor leadership of Sikhs has led to this decline. If a leader does come to the fore he/she is usually easily maligned by the politics and they drift back into the mainstream of the normal political groups or completely disappear due to being quashed.

The current position of Punjab isn't the normality or peace that Sikhs or Punjabis aspire to. There is much work to be done in Punjab by Sikhs, Hindus and the state and central governments.

Short-term thinking and short-term politics needs to be weeded out. It will only take one inspirational and charismatic leader like Bhindranwale to point out the above issues to Sikhs en masse and we could be right back to a pre-1984 deadlock.

The warning signs are glaring at us, with flashing neon lights – when will we awake to the dangers of

Punjab's future? Sikhs inside and outside of Punjab, need to all become responsible and take up the baton and share the workload in regenerating Punjab. The fortunes of Punjab are in the hands of Punjabis, both in India and in the diaspora, after all, they will be the ones picking up the pieces, if it all goes horribly wrong again.

Relevance of Khalistan

"Today the Sikh community has spread far beyond its homeland in Punjab, India, and exists in diaspora across the world. The expansion of the diaspora and the elevation of the demand for an independent Sikh state of Khalistan have occurred in tandem..."[227]

Cynthia Mahmood (2001: 7)

Support in the diaspora for Khalistan is still strong. Sikhs outside of India do not have to fear reprisals from the Indian state for their freedoms of expression, although prominent Khalistani Sikhs or critics of India, do still encounter problems obtaining entry visas to India.

Pictures of martyrs of Khalistan are portrayed in Gurdwaras throughout the globe and there is a glorification of the sacrifices of these Sikhs, at many major festivals. The UK hosts the biggest annual protest march against the Indian state in June. It commemorates those that died in Operation Blue Star and is a public rally to raise the demands of justice, freedom and truth for Sikhs in India. Each year, between 10,000 to 30,000 Sikhs attend this march, which commences at Hyde Park and ends with a rally at Trafalgar Square.

On a macro level, the Sikh community fought a civil war of secession against the Indian state between the years of 1985 – 1995. I purposely say 1985, as the events of 1984 were too colossal and the extreme repression of Sikhs meant that a re-grouping had to take place. With the end of the civil war a peaceful lull developed.

Many accuse Sikhs in the West for still promoting the vision for Khalistan and disturbing the peace in India. Nevertheless, "Raj Karega Khalsa" is still stated on a

---

[227] *A sea of Orange*, Cynthia Mahmood

daily basis in Sikh homes and Gurdwaras throughout India. The spirit of Khalistan resonates throughout the globe wherever Sikhs conduct their supplication prayer in which they repeat this statement (Raj Karega Khalsa – The Khalsa shall rule).

The right to self-determination is enshrined in international law by the United Nations Charter and the 1966 International Covenant on Civil and Political Rights. Article 1 of the 1966 Covenant reads: *"All peoples have the right of self-determination. By virtue of that right they freely determine their political status and freely pursue their economic, social and cultural development"*. Thus the pursuit of Khalistan is supported by international law.

Interestingly, whilst India has formally signed up to the 1966 Covenant, it has formally informed the UN that it does not accept that the right of self-determination applies to the nations or peoples within India. The UN's Human Rights Committee has asked India to withdraw that 'reservation' but India refuses to do so.

Sikhs in the Punjab have been through a torrid experience in the last thirty years, thus demands for self-determination are no longer at the fore for them. The reality of the current situation within Punjab is that Sikhs residing there, are no longer interested in the demand for Khalistan – it is a distant dream. Some political parties do still raise the claim but they have very little political or popular support.

Protagonists of Khalistan argue it should be based on a geographical rule over the current day Punjab and adjoining Punjabi speaking areas in India; others believe it should also include Punjab in Pakistan. Others extend the geographical realms and argue Khalistan should include all historical Gurdwaras be that Nanded in the South, Lahore in Pakistan or Patna in the East. At the very least, they argue some sort of steps towards granting Amritsar a holy city status[228] should be made. This was part of the original demands of the Anandpur Sahib Resolution.[229]

Previous Sikh Sovereign states have existed on a macro level, thus Khalistan is factually based in Sikh History, theology and prophecy. The Sikhs fought a war of secession recently and the right to self-determination is universal.

Most Sikhs are ambiguous on what this Khalistan should be and today the majority have little commitment to fulfilling its realization. People will always choose peace over war, unless they are forced to defend themselves. Therefore, Khalistan is not an immediate priority for most Sikhs and is rather a distant dream of something that may occur in the future.

The micro level observations of Khalistan are still of significance as is the spirit of Khalistan. The spirit of Khalistan lives on in Sikhs, as their history, ideology and morals make them an independent nation, which will always raise its voice and arms, if needed to fight oppression and gain freedom(s). So Sikhs are intrinsically Khalistani. This may not transfer to macro politics and mobilising the masses to fight for an independent state, but on an individual basis it will mean fighting against all types

---

[228] Holy City Status would entail a ban on alcohol and tobacco in Amritsar or at the very least in a cordoned area near to the Harmander Sahib. Hardwar a religious centre for Hindus has a ban on non-vegetarian foods and alcohol throughout the city – Sikhs aspire for a similar ruling. Although this status could also be achieved through the Punjabi state government and the Sikhs should really pursue this through the Akali Dal (the Sikh Political Party which is currently in power in Punjab.)

[229] See the Anandpur Sahib Resolution at Appendix 2

of inequality and oppression in all walks of life and for humanitarian causes for the whole of mankind.

Today, many Sikhs from the disapora travel regularly to India. They may have lived alongside and socialized with Khalistanis, whom do want secession. They may be Khalistani's in the broader sense that they believe Khalsa Raaj (rule of the Khalsa) will prevail. They may be contributing to the realisation of this dream by raising awareness about the oppression of Sikhs and may be teaching others about Sikh history, theology and polity. So, on an individual basis they are carrying on the fight for Khalistan.

On a personal and individual level 'Khalistan' can be argued to be the experience of the glow of freedom. Hence some may argue that they actually live in a kind of Khalistan in the UK. How is this so? If I am not oppressed and discriminated against, then on an individual basis this may be Khalistan for me. Now, this view of Khalistan is what may resonate for a lot of people today. This is where some Sikhs who live in India argue against a geographically confined Khalistan. Some fortunate Sikhs in India may go through their lives without being oppressed or discriminated against. Hence they cannot see the relevance of secession.

When we view Article 25 of the Indian constitution it states that Sikhs are Hindus; this lack of individual identity along with Punjab being discriminated against in distribution of its river waters and the countless grievances, give reasons for the feeling of oppression for Sikhs in India on a macro level. Thus Sikhs are still discriminated against and these discriminations can lead to future revivals of separatist tendencies. The realisation of Khalistan is a distant dream but the issues which led to its declaration and revival as a Sikh ideal state have not been addressed and could easily lead to future revivals.

Therefore, the dichotomy that exists of Khalistan, is a macro and micro one. An individual can experience 'Khalistan' if he/she is free and treated as an equal citizen. Parity of rights and freedom are the crux of the debate. On a macro level however, these micro observations may be overlooked, due to discrimination against Sikhs in legislation, justice, equality and freedom. Thus the demand for Khalistan will keep raising its head in front of national security until such a time that Khalistan is realized, or is no longer needed.

Conclusion

30 years after 1984, I sit here writing this - the concluding chapter of this book, which has entailed a search of reason and facts. I'll admit, that at times my pen dropped from my hand and I couldn't write any more. Too much blood has irrigated the land of Punjab. Too much blood has become embedded into the marble at Harmander Sahib. Too many lives lost. Innocence of youth lost. For what? A frenzy of violence played out in the hope of a better tomorrow.

Regardless of where you stand politically – whosoever engaged in these acts of violence, did so, to appease their own principles of righteousness. The Punjab Police collected bounties and did their job and met their objectives. The Sikh militants fought for faith and nation. The orchestrated mobs, killed, raped and displaced Sikhs with disturbing meticulousness. Those in power – the politicians, engineered the loss of lives, through tactics they thought would lead to re-election. These are now chapters of history, but the scars are still fresh, as are many of the characters involved – they still live with their experiences and memories of these years.

I will now start to bring my thoughts to a close. We need to consider why the insurgency began and how it came to an end. From my research on the topic, I think the insurgency was a reactionary one and not a pro-active one, in that it reacted to the actions of the state and central government. The Sikhs did not pro-actively start an insurgent movement and the central government dictated the timing of the end of the insurgency.

Human rights issues still persist and the chances of justice or redress for victims look slim. The post colonial era has continued where it left off, trade is still the primary concern. Violence in Punjab and outside of India, will probably continue in relation to the pursuit of Indian officials who have committed crimes against Sikhs.

Sikhs and their Khalistani aspirations are now labelled within the 'war on terror' by some state governments and Sikhs are watched, if they seem to be 'extreme.' Todays Punjab, has multiple issues to address and Sikhs in the diaspora need to support the resolution of these problems to avoid future calamities. I have purposely only touched upon these issues here and I will now tackle them sequentially.

Starting and ending an insurgency

Pre-1984 politics was about creating a moral panic, of a threat of Sikh Separatism and terrorism. Only two Sikh groups had flouted the idea of Khalistan before 1984 and were fringe movements, the Dal Khalsa and Council of Khalistan.

The spectre of terrorism had been spread through the mass media, but the facts counteract that there was a real threat. So I conclude that this was all politically engineered by Indira Gandhi to quell the threat of Sikhs - who had challenged her authority during the emergency, and was used as a tool for electioneering. She worked in the hope of getting mass support of the Hindu majority of India to grow her fame as someone who can quash movements of dissidence; to be seen as a saviour of the Indian nation, as she had done so, with the war with Pakistan in 1971, leading to Bangladeshi independence. She did this astutely, but she had underestimated the prowess of the Sikh faith.

Anyone who has attacked Harmander Sahib has always died within 153 days of the attack[230] and as the one who called the operation, she had to follow in the historical steps of other invaders of the shrine. Indira Gandhi's actions meant that she would also follow the footsteps of other aggressors and she was assassinated as a result.

These policies of creating a spectre of Sikh terrorism led to a self-fulfilling prophecy and Sikhs actually started fulfilling the role that had been projected of them. Many had no choice but to take to arms in defence. Theses Sikhs had to choose between defending themselves or accept the harsh realities of arrest, harassment and torture indefinitely.

Nobody chooses to take to arms and fight for independence lightly – these insurgents put their lives on the line everyday for themselves and their community, as they saw this as the only hope of living their lives with dignity. There were wrongs done on both sides, by the Punjab Police and the Sikh insurgents – some Sikhs took to being racist against Hindus and some still do, even though Sikh teachings are clearly against this.

No Sikh would oppress anyone, let alone a Hindu, and the killings of Hindus in India were not disproportionate to their population in Punjab, 61% of those that died were Sikhs. *"Of a total of 11,694 persons killed by terrorists in Punjab during the period 1981 – 1993, 7,139 – more than 61 per cent - were Sikhs."*[231] The

---

[230] This refers to five attacks on Harmander Sahib, in which the shrine has been defiled and/or destroyed – where the desecration was extreme. See http://dailysikhupdates.com/2013/08/17/153-days-after-attacking-harmandir-sahib/ The complex was attacked in 1986 and 1988 also by the Indian security forces but there was hardly any blood-shed and no shots were fired at the Harmander Sahib. So this statistic refers directly to those invasions where the clear objective was to crush the Sikhs.

[231] KPS Gill in Knights of Falsehood, www.satp.org/satporgtp/publication/nightsoffalsehood/falsehood4.htm

total numbers that died during these years will never be known empirically, the estimates range from 100,000 – 250,000 plus.

Also the depraved nature of politics is hinted at by KPS Gill and Kirpal Dhillon (both ex-chiefs of Punjab Police), who point out that the insurgency was probably allowed to run on, to serve political interests. Thus, a callous disregard for human life took place.

KPS Gill when speaking of the policing situation in 1988 states, *"What had been lacking was a clear mandate, and a freedom to carry on the battle without crippling political interference."*[232] He got this clear mandate later and that's how he became to be known by Sikhs all over the globe as the 'butcher of Punjab' and was termed 'Supercop' by the Indian press for his achievements in crushing the insurgency. He further elaborates, *"In 1989 we had reduced terrorism, confined it in thirteen police districts out of 220 -230. The terrorists were sending us messages by March 1989 – 'Please give us a way out and we will lay down our arms.'*[233] He says that he sent a message to the Indian Intelligence Bureau in March 1989 outlining the current position in their war against the insurgents. He elaborates further of why he thinks the residual insurgency was allowed to fester, *"I think it was a political decision, I think, that this residual terrorism should be allowed to remain until the election ... this was the crux of the Congress campaign. As the elections approached they said, right, now talk to the terrorists ... The terrorists wanted a formula which allowed them to lay down weapons without conceding defeat. In turn, the*

---

[232] ibid
[233] Fernandes (2006: 246-247) *Holy Warriors,* Portobello Books, London

government wanted to make security and peace in Punjab an election issue."[234]

Subsequently though, Rajiv Gandhi still lost in the election and a new government was formed under the leadership of Chandar Shakra and KPS Gill was transferred back to Delhi. He got reposted as the DGP of Punjab Police in November 1991, when the Congress party came back to power nationally under Narismha Rao, and it was very soon after that the insurgency had been crushed; it was bought to an end by early 1993.

Kirpal Dhillon argues that one theory about the abrupt ending of the insurgency was that the police and security forces actually had a grip on the movement and had infiltrated it at all levels. Thus, when the political decision was made to end it, the curtain was pulled down, with devastating precision and in a matter of months the insurgency was brought to an end.[235] KPS Gill's comments earlier also point to this possibility. This agenda would have suited the Punjab Police as well, as they could allow the notoriety of insurgents to grow, which would in turn increase the bounties offered for their heads, and so they would financially benefit from the insurgency continuing.

However, the insurgents had the last say, in 1995 the Congress Party Chief Minister of Punjab, Beant Singh was killed in a bombing in Chandigarh. This proved that the insurgent groups still had access to high profile targets and the fire power to match. But peace has been the consistent mode of Punjab since 1995 and the insurgent groups have mostly fallen into disarray and no strategic target of theirs has fallen prey to their bullets since 1995.

---

[234] Fernandes (2006: 247) *Holy Warriors*, Portobello Books, London
[235] Dhillon (2006) *Identity and Survival, Sikh Militancy in India 1978-1993*. Penguin Books, Delhi.

Human Rights

"The generous tributes showered upon the Punjab police and its chief for their singular success in containing one of the world's most lethal militant movements tended to briefly eclipse the magnitude of illegal actions and atrocities committed by the security forces during that dark decade. However, when the full facts came to public notice, there was widespread outrage, revulsion and indignation in India and abroad."[236] The revulsion may have followed in circles of civil liberty in India, but very little was, and is done, in terms of following the rule of law and putting these wrongs, right.

The 'greater good' of saving the Indian nation is seen as primary and the loss of innocent lives secondary. The dehumanization of lives of Punjabis and more so, those of Sikhs, had and has become deep-seated, with no change in this being foreseeable.

Asia Watch, a human rights agency reported that, *"Throughout Punjab, torture is practiced systematically in Police stations, in prisons and in the detention camps used by the paramilitary forces. In virtually every case Asia Watch investigated, persons taken into custody were tortured. Methods of torture include:*

- *Pulling the victim's legs far apart so as to cause great pain and internal pelvic injury*
- *Rotating a heavy wooden or metal roller over the victim's thighs. Policemen frequently sit or stand on the roller to increase the weight. In some cases,*

---

[236] Dhillon (2006: 348) *Identity and Survival, Sikh Militancy in India 1978-1993.* Penguin Books, Delhi.

> *the roller is placed behind the victims knees and the legs forced back over it, crushing against the roller*
> - *Electric shock, applied to the victim's genitals, head, ears and legs*
> - *Prolonged beating with canes or leather straps*
> - *Tying the victim's hands behind the back and suspending him or her from the ceiling by the arms*
> - *Rape, threats of rape or molestation.*"[237]

The dangers of impunity of these police brutalities were aptly summarized by the UN, *"Measures taken by Governments to open independent and impartial investigations with a view to identifying and bringing to justice those responsible for human rights violations constitute one of the main pillars of the effective protection of human rights. Consequently, a climate of impunity for human rights violators contributes to a great extent to the persistence of - and sometimes even an increase in - human rights abuses in a number of countries."*[238]

The impunity of the Punjab Police led to them continuing their corrupt practices, even after the end of the insurgency, which meant more misery for the Punjab public. For those who unfortunately get embroiled in criminal cases; bribes, corruption and torture are still common place.

In 1999 Amnesty International made a number of recommendations to the Indian government about the above, the salient points are quoted here, *"The Government of India should fully implement its obligations under international law with respect to allegations of human rights violations in Punjab committed between 1984 and*

---

[237] *Human Rights in India: Punjab in Crisis,* An Asian Watch Report, New York, 1991, p.5
[238] UN Special Rapporteur on extrajudicial, summary or arbitrary executions, 1993 report, paragraph 686

1994. Specifically it should ensure independent and impartial investigation of all allegations of human rights violations; the right of victims to receive redress and reparation; and that those identified as being suspected of perpetrating human rights violations are brought to justice in trials which meet international standards for fairness ... The State Government of Punjab should make a commitment that illegal practices carried out by the Punjab police in past years will not be tolerated and that those suspected of such practices will be prosecuted in accordance with law..."[239]

The current DGP of Punjab Police is Sumedh Saini – he has pending criminal cases for the abduction and disappearance of two people, dating back to 1994.[240] Saini served throughout the period of militancy and many Sikhs have gone on record to say he has tortured them. The same officer's who committed atrocities still hold positions of power, although the rule of law could still catch up with them. With the passage of time and delayed proceedings, the trials usually bear little results as witnesses have either died, disappeared or don't show up, out of fear. So once the accused officers or politicians do finally get to the dock in court, they are exonerated; adding to the frustration and agony of families affected.

Harmander Sahib – The Golden Temple Today

All the signs of Operation Blue Star have been removed from the complex and most visitors today, wouldn't believe that the shrine witnessed one of the

---

[239] *"A vital opportunity to end impunity in Punjab"* p.16, Amnesty International, August 1999, AI Index: ASA 20/24/99

[240] http://timesofindia.indiatimes.com/city/chandigarh/court-puts-trial-in-saini-case-on-fast-track/articleshow/30872017.cms

bloodiest battles in modern Indian history. The Akaal Takhat has been reconstructed and extensive works around the complex have repaired most of the damage. Although blood has become embedded, at certain points, in the marble in the walkway (parkarma), as reported by Mark Tully in a BBC radio documentary in 2004.

Each year on 6th June, a "Ghallughara Divas" is organized, which loosely translates to – 'day of the holocaust'. The main function takes places at the Akaal Takhat where families of defenders of the shrine are honoured.

More recently a memorial has been constructed, in memory of those who died whilst defending the complex against the Indian Army. There was much controversy about its construction in the Indian media, but regardless of the controversy, it now stands within the confines of the complex. However, it is a little disappointing to see that this memorial fails to serve its function; to list the dead, and no attempts to collate a list of 'all' those who died has been made.

Progress isn't likely in regaining the lost Sikh artifacts' of the Harmander Sahib Library. Accusations of the contents being stored in Bihar in an army cantonment are rife and a legal case has been pending since Operation Blue Star. This treasure of Sikh History seems to be doomed to being lost.

The Indian government after Operation Blue Star and subsequent raids on the complex, made a strategic plan to ensure ease of access to the complex by security forces. Today, a garden area surrounds most of the perimeter of the complex (Ghalliara) – this was constructed by the government after razing all adjoining buildings. Houses and businesses were purchased by the state and the garden has been constructed with military and intelligence planners; to ensure an easy access to the shrine and protection of security forces through this garden. Thus, the garden is not a simple garden but a carefully designed one; it will protect incoming forces from anyone inside, if fired upon. Currently, the last phase of this project is being constructed, with the massive overhaul of the entrance area of the complex through the clock tower.

Post Colonial era

Sikhs came to Great Britain in the 1960's and have continued to do so, since. Many Sikhs now have second and third generations in the United Kingdom. So a strong association between India and Great Britain exists for them.

During the years of militancy, a Conservative Member of Parliament Terry Dicks of Hayes and Harlington, took up the Sikh cause. In a debate on 29th November 1991 – at the House of Commons, he made the following statement about the moral responsibility of Britain in the Sikh cause. *"In 1947, when India obtained its independence, it was the British who accepted a guarantee by the Hindus, who made 84 per cent of the population that the self determination of the Sikhs in the Punjab would be recognised. On this basis, the British Government granted India its independence. Unfortunately for the Sikhs, the British Government has done nothing to enforce the guarantee and successive congress party dominated Government's here and has been able to ignore the pledge. The failure of the Indian Government, aided and abetted by Britain, to help keep their word has led the Sikh people to call upon their own independent state."*[241] This raises the question of the moral obligations of the British state in terms of Sikh issues; for their Sikh constituents in the UK and their families in a commonwealth state.

Sikhs who were involved in the separatist movement of Khalistan and reside in the UK, openly talk about being tracked and spied upon by intelligence agencies of the UK and India. At no point has Britain acknowledged the events of 1984 as a genocide and mixed support from MP's is received in bilateral issues with India and the Sikhs. However, recently Sikhs have become more politically astute and are now engaging with parliamentarians and the state institutions.

Many Sikhs love their British identity and the fact that they are free to practice their faith and wear their articles of faith, especially the Kirpan (ceremonial dagger) without impediment. The Sikhs are recognized as a racial and religious group in British law, thus, British Sikhs have more rights than their counterparts in India. So many a Sikh in Britain has more allegiance with Britain than India, as they are free to live and practice their faith, here in the UK.

Recent disclosures from the UK government archives have caused many Sikhs to question their identity. The disclosures prove that the British government provided military advice to the Indian government about Operation Blue Star – in simple terms the British government of the day were privy to the plan to attack the Sikh Vatican – to what extent they agreed with it, is open to the public to judge. William Hague the current Home Secretary gave a statement and admitted files had been lost – so the truth

---

[241] Professor J.S Grewal, Sikh Identity, the Akalis & Khalistan, an essay in Punjab in Prosperity and Violence, Chandigarh 1998.

once again in its entirety, has been lost or covered up. The statement by him acknowledged that the British government gave advice, which differed from what was actually implemented and the British were not consulted again prior to the army assault.[242]

This recent interaction with the British government and India in 1984, has meant many young Sikhs are questioning their nationality and identity. The reality, that they are a homeless nation, is being brought to the fore; India and Britain are now both questioned as true homes. These Sikhs feel like nomads in an international community, where they are questioning which governments actually support their freedoms and faith, in the truest sense.

Trade is what led Britain to make India a colony and trade is still a major feature of the relationship or the primary factor. Recently when the recession started in Britain, student visas were purposely relaxed to lure foreign students to Britain, to pay fees and enrol on courses. This ensured two things, a fresh income stream to fund and support the failing economy and provide cheap and sometimes illegal labour, as most students would work longer hours than their visas allowed.

A lot of these foreign students came from ex-colonies and Punjabis from India flooded the student market, in the long term hope of financial advancement. However, what actually happened with many is that they

---

[242] See the full statement by William Hague at this link
https://www.gov.uk/government/speeches/statement-on-the-indian-operation-at-sri-harmandir-sahib-in-1984

found it very difficult to find work and became even worse off financially, or had to work at extortionately low rates.

Those that could afford to return home to Punjab went back and those that couldn't became illegal immigrants. Some are homeless and destitute. Thus, these individuals were also exploited through this post-colonial relationship. The lure of Britain for these migrants is for economical advancement and to become permanently settled in the UK. For many who were granted these student visas this was never a possibility, as they were granted short-term visas, with little chance of extension of their visas or permanent residency.

The nexus of continuing violence
The risk of future violence is still prevalent in the minds of many and was aptly demonstrated in 2012 when Lieutenant General Kuldip Brar visited London. He had been one of the four generals leading Operation Blue Star. He was attacked by four Sikhs, four males and a female (who provided tactical support). These five Sikhs were later all found guilty of Grievous Bodily Harm (GBH) with intent. In what was a poor effort to cause serious harm, Brar escaped with minimal injuries.

This case highlighted the continuing anger against officers of the Indian state who attacked the Sikhs Vatican. Whilst violence is not condoned in British society and law, one has to acknowledge the mitigating circumstances. They were attacking somebody that they all viewed as a mass murderer, much like other war criminals, such as Mugabe.

We can assess this attack on General Brar in a wider light of British law and society. Tony Blair as the Prime

Minister ordered the British troops into Iraq on the premise of weapons of mass destruction and he did not face criminal charges – then where is the parity in law for these four Sikhs? Tony Blair's Cabinet approval, for the Iraq war, is a culpable humanitarian crime, as it led most importantly to the deaths of our loyal service men and women, let alone innocent Iraqis. Similarly, as has been proven by eye witness testimonies and post-mortems; cold-blooded murders were committed by the Indian army in Operation Blue Star led by General Brar.

The above argument of mitigating circumstances in this criminal case hasn't received much attention; rather the media has chosen to pursue the official line of Brar and his protests that no killing of innocent people took place in Operation Blue Star.

General Brar also made some unfounded accusations about the radicalisation of Sikh youth in the UK and elsewhere, alleging this radicalisation has led to him being attacked by people who were very young in 1984. The attackers were all in their mid-30's and contrary to what General Brar said in his interview[243] that these attackers have been radicalised by their upbringing in the UK - the actual fact of the matter is that all his attackers, are actually Indian born and bred. All five of them at the time of the attack, had only been in the UK for a maximum of 7 years – so there was no British upbringing for them.

One of the attackers lost his father and brother in the 1984 army attack, so he had a clear motive. The other four attackers were probably incited by Brar's actions, that they would have learnt of whilst in India. General Brar's

---

[243] BBC Asian Network, Nihal, *Lt-Gen Brar talks about his attackers sentencing*, http://www.bbc.co.uk/programmes/p01n6qh0

accusation of radicalisation and extremism in this case of UK Sikh Youth is unfounded and unproven.

The vengeance for 1984 continues, hence incidents like the Brar attack. The perpetrators of state orchestrated violence against the Sikhs are protected with the utmost security protocols in India and the threat of violence will continue until the day they die.

Terrorism & Sikhs

The 9/11 attacks on the twin towers, created a panic in governments to now tackle the spectre of terrorism. The cold war ended and the new war is now against sporadic terrorist strikes. This new war, led to the proscription of two organisations in the USA and UK – they are the Babbar Khalsa International (BKI) and the International Sikh Youth Federation (ISYF) – both were banned as terrorist organisations in the UK in 2001.

It must be noted that these two organisations had registered offices and branches throughout the UK spanning from 1984 – 2001. The executive members of the ISYF had mingled with Tony Blair in 1999 as the Sikhs celebrated the tercentenary of the Khalsa. One of the ISYF members had received an OBE on the recommendation of Tony Blair.

So now in the UK – after the banning of these organisations and the new war on terror – the spotlight of terrorism has also fallen onto Sikh individuals and their organisations. In Turbanology[244] Jay Sohal and I set out the misconceptions about Sikh identity due to the Sikh

---

[244] Sohal (2013), *Turbanology Guide to Sikh Identity*, Dot Hyphen, Birmingham

turban and what this has meant, with the war on terror, for Sikhs across the globe.

However, after the proscription of BKI and ISYF, none of their previous members have been arrested for any offences and their memberships have just reorganised into different organisations and nearly all of the leading personalities of BKI and ISYF, are now engaged fully in the political system in the UK with Parliamentarians and local councillors.

India Today & Sikhs in the Diaspora

Today, Sikhs that were involved in the insurgency languish in Indian jails. Some of the cases of these prisoners have become very prominent. Balwant Singh Rajoana admitted his involvement in the bombing that killed the Chief Minister of Punjab in 1995 – he is now on death row, even though he has already served 17 years. In effect, he has already served a life sentence, but still faces the possibility of the death penalty. His execution received temporary reprieve in 2012 after a campaign to halt it, received some success.

The campaign to halt Rajoanas hanging received world-wide support from the Sikhs and has once again brought the issues of Sikh rights in India, to the fore. Rajoana successfully espoused his political views through the media, which has made him an iconic Sikh figure of the modern era.

During the height of the campaign to quash Rajoana's hanging – peaceful protests were held throughout India and the diaspora. One of these protests took place in Gurdaspur in which the Punjab Police shot dead Japsal Singh on 29th March 2012 who had been peacefully protesting. He became a martyr and his family was honoured by the Sikh leadership but there is no hope of justice in the investigation into finding the guilty officer who shot him. A case is lodged with the Punjab Police, but there is neither the political will of the current Sikh leaders or the Punjab government, currently led by a Sikh – Parkash Singh Badal, to bring the culprit(s) to the dock and get a conviction.

Similarly, Darshan Singh Lohara was shot dead in 2009 whilst peacefully protesting against the cultist Ashutosh's organisation in Ludhiana. Once again no justice in law is expected for the offending murderer.

Davinderpal Singh Bhullar is also on death row. He was deported from Germany and subsequently found guilty of a bombing. In his criminal case, none of the witnesses of the prosecution identified him. The only incriminating evidence was an uncorroborated confessional statement which was later retracted. Nonetheless, he has been incarcerated since 1995 and has been on death row since 2001. He is in prison in the notorious Tihar Jail and has subsequently become mentally unstable due to his ordeal (of being on death row for more than a decade). His case is now under review and he has been saved from the death penalty and his hanging has been commuted to life imprisonment. His case is also of international prominence.

In 2013, Bhai Gurbaksh Singh Khalsa started a hunger strike in India to peacefully protest about Sikh prisoners who have served life sentences, but have no hope of being freed. His hunger strike became international news and achieved temporary reprieve, on parole, for some prisoners who have already served life[245]. But all those freed on parole have returned to prison. He has now started a movement to free all those who have already served life sentences to be freed from prisons throughout India – Sikhs and non-Sikhs alike.

The latent issues of the militancy continue today. Current Sikh concerns are centred on discrimination with their ex-militants whom are imprisoned and justice for normal Sikhs, who had been peacefully protesting for a Sikh cause and were murdered by the Punjab Police.

The feelings of discrimination against Sikhs spill over when cases like that of Kishori Lal come to prominence. Kishori Lal was convicted of killing 3 Sikhs in Delhi in the anti-Sikh pogroms. His sentence was commuted from the death sentence to life imprisonment. His sentence was then cut short and he was subsequently freed.[246] The Sikhs ask why this isn't the case for Rajoana and Bhullar. Anecdotal discrimination in high profile cases continues, which is continuing to grow seeds of dissension and discord amongst Sikhs – this is peacefully portrayed at the moment, through protests and petitions.

Peaceful movements can become violent ones, when no progress through peaceful means is in sight. This has been the Sikh way in history; to first peacefully agitate and then take to arms when justice cannot be achieved through peaceful means and their revolutionary identity is under threat of being eliminated. Unfortunately, the current position is that, *"...though militancy and extremist violence have been eliminated, deep-seated political grievances remain unresolved. What was needed was a mature,*

---

[245] Life being more than 15 years imprisonment
[246] http://archive.indianexpress.com/news/human-rights-group-questions-early-release-of-kishori-lal/913580/

informed and statesmanlike approach to unravel the root cause of the upsurge, traits in dire need of replacement in Indian political classes."

We've got a Sikh Prime Minister and a Sikh party in power in Punjab – the Akali Dal of Parkash Singh Badal. Surely there are no problems of political discord, in Sikhs, in India now? It is with regret that I have to write, that regardless of Sikhs holding positions of power today, or in 1984, the latent issues of Sikh freedoms and rights continue, as do the socio-economical challenges of the Punjab. It may indeed take another 30 years to solve these issues, which could only occur through a strong politically willed leadership – none of which, I see at the moment in India or Punjab. The newly formed Aam Aadmi Party seems like an idealist party and one that may bring the much needed social reforms – but only time will tell, of how successful and effective they can become.

I fear that the destruction I have witnessed, which has affected so many lives, still represents a simmering pot. Now, destiny will decide if that pot is turned off and cooled or that it overflows and takes over the lives of many once again. Choose peace not war. But, **"When all peaceful means have been exhausted, it is just to draw the sword."**[247]

---

[247] Guru Gobind Singh – the 10th Sikh Guru

My Reflections

I don't like the memories because the tears come easily, and once again I break my promise to myself for this day. It's a constant battle. A war between remembering and forgetting.[248]

The above quote aptly introduces my emotions on the discussions of this book. I am a tortured soul, who has witnessed, heard and studied the effects of the last 30 years. I have seen the tears, hatred, torture and vengeance that it has created. I have cried and still do, when I think of these events. Writing this book has been a struggle as I am very passionate about the topics I have written about.

What compelled me to write this book was a short speech of Bhai Jaswant Singh Khalra[249] in which he describes the effect of one small lantern challenging the darkness. Bhai Jaswant Singh Khalra became this lamp that challenged the darkness of the Punjab Police in its extra-judicial killings of the Sikhs. He argued that we should all become lanterns and when we collectively converge the darkness will end. This darkness is the truth, justice and freedom that is veiled in the events of the last 30 years.

As a humble and insignificant Sikh, I am also attempting to become one of these lanterns. Whereas Bhai Jaswant Singh Khalra challenged the system of darkness directly, I have merely written a book. Nonetheless, I was compelled in a similar vein to write.

If my voice shakes when I speak of these atrocities or my pens falls from my hand, I will still endeavour to

---

[248] Quotation taken from http://theirgraves.tumblr.com/post/19326727678
[249] You can hear this short speech here in English and Punjabi http://www.youtube.com/watch?v=Mcux1JlxJOw

voice the truth about these events and not deter from the glorious history of great souls before me, who did not flinch in their pursuits of justice. I hope and pray that I can be true to this cause which can be treacherous at times.

Those that know me and have read my other title on the same topic, 'Game of Love' may be surprised by the objective nature of this book. After 30 years I feel this is how, 'we', the Sikhs, need to now, intellectually tackle the issues. I am horrified at times at the minimalistic knowledge that 'we' as Sikhs have on this recent history. Each Sikh should be armed with the knowledge about these events and have the capacity to promote the truth in an intellectual manner. The Sikhs are after all a nation led by 'learning' as taught by the Gurus.

I hope this book can go some way to arming Sikhs and the world with the knowledge and truth of what went on and is currently occurring.

Harjinder Singh
(Walsall, United Kingdom)

Acknowledgements

Writing any book is a daunting task, this was no different. This book was a team effort and I must acknowledge the input of those that gave critical appraisals and feedback. Also those that helped with the research and fact finding need to be acknowledged.

I will now list the names of those that helped in alphabetical order. I am indebted to them for helping complete this book. Amandip Kaur, Amanjyot Kaur, Amerdip Kaur, Angela Steatham, Baljinder Kaur, Dr Gurnam Singh, Harpartap Singh, Jasmeet Singh, Navjot Kaur, Rajvinder Kaur, Ranjit Singh Srai, Sonia Kaur and Upjeet Kaur.

I thank God for blessing us all with this voluntary work and I hope Akaal Publishers can continue to produce literary titles that have profound effects on people's lives.

Appendices

Appendix 1 – Declaration of Khalistan

[250]"Victory Be In The Name Of One God"
Sri Akal Takht Sahib, Amritsar.
Five Member Panthak Committee

The Panth Khalsa[251], founded by Sahib Sri Guru Gobind Singh Ji on the Baisakhi of 1699 AD, once again as per the saying of Dhar Tej Krara (be a brave and glorious warrior) and as per Guru's ordained dictum, 'Raj Karega Khalsa' (the Khalsa shall rule), through the Five member Panthak Committee nominated by the Sarbat Khalsa on 26th January, 1986, fulfils the most cherished dream of the Sikhs (by this declaration) of 'Khalistan'.

On this auspicious day, from the Holy Akal Takht Sahib, it is (on behalf of the five member Panthak Committee) hereby declared before all the States/Governments and notified to them that from today onwards, the Khalsa Panth will have its own Home, 'Khalistan', wherein will ever remain high in the air the flags, towers and posts of the Sikhs, and wherein the writ of the Khalsa will run supreme. Herein the entire control of the government and administration shall be vested in those that pray for the welfare of all and earn their livelihood by the sweat of labour.

The slogan of 'Khalistan', which has been moving the hearts of the Sikhs and the Sikh youths for several years and the founding of which had been mentioned by Sant Baba Jarnail Singh Ji Khalsa Bhindranwale, on June 3, 1984 at the time of the military attack on Sri Darbar

---

[250] Original declaration taken from http://shaheed-khalsa.com/declaration.html revisions of errors in typing, translation and referencing by the author on 9/2/14
[251] Khalsa Nation. Panth means nation

Sahib and Sri Akal Takht Sahib by the Hindu[252] Government of India. The Sikh Sangat had ratified this idea with great joy and thrill at the time of the Sarbat Khalsa convened on April 13, 1986. The Sikh Sangats repeat their commitment to the dictum 'The Khalsa shall rule' in their daily prayer but it is today, that by unbounded grace of the Guru, the commitment to 'Khalistan' is being realised. The Five member Panthak Committee constituted by the Sarbat Khalsa convened by the Damdami Taksal, today hereby declares (the formation of) 'Khalistan'.

This declaration of Khalistan is made before the Khalsa Panth as well as the Sikh community (comprising of every Sikh; male, female, mother, brother etc.) so that all of us may, in accordance with our individual capacity, contribute to its cause physically, mentally, and financially and may thus prove worthy of our exalted Guru's saying of, *"The death of brave heroes is blessed, if it is approved by God"*[253]. Today the five member Panthak Committee calls upon the entire Sikh nation to be ready for all types of sufferings and sacrifices.

The wish of the Khalsa is to achieve the declared objective by the Guru's grace, love and affection. Our programme is:

No one is our enemy and no one is stranger to us, all are our brethren[254]

We are not interested in creating any upheaval or in shedding undue blood and we expect the same from others too. We express our firm faith in resolving all the issues

---

[252] Hindu is mentioned here, due to the Hindu majority who in effect rule the country. India is also commonly referred to as Hindustan the land of the Hindus
[253] Guru Nanak, 579, Raag Vadhans, Sri Guru Granth Sahib
[254] Guru Arjan Dev, 1299, Raag Kaanara, Sri Guru Granth Sahib

cordially and through a dialogue with the Hindu majority and the Government of India. We hope that the Government of India will not be blinded by an anti-Sikh attitude underlying Brahminism and will face the reality by giving recognition to the formation of 'Khalistan'. This would be the real Satyagraha of Bharat[255].

Political Recognition

The Khalsa Panth demands political recognition (of 'Khalistan') from all the powers of the world, especially America (U.S.A.), England, Pakistan, China, Canada, West Germany and from the Governments which are signatory to the Warsaw Pact, and Italy, France, Japan, Sri Lanka, Nepal, Burma, Bhutan, Bangladesh, Iran, Iraq, Saudi-Arabia, Israel, Equador etc. We also appeal to the member countries of U.N.O. to grant us recognition, help and assistance for the various political, military and other issues, which have arisen or may arise concerning the human rights in 'Khalistan'.

We are hopeful that the new government of 'Khalistan' will be formed soon, but the Panth is seeking its political recognition to avoid problems that may be caused by the delay in its recognition. We have already demanded recognition by the Government of India, which should come forth, in order to keep good neighbourly relations (between India and 'Khalistan') that will help in restoring peace and brotherhood in Punjab, as well as in India, and encouraging toleration so as to end all bitterness of the day.

---

[255] Satyargraha means insistence of truth. In this insistence it means that true peace can be achieved by the foundation of Khalistan as a country. Bharat is an ancient name for India, Bharat was a King who ruled the subcontinent.

Since 'Khalistan' has come into being, the Government of India should (recognising its existence) take political, military and administrative measures such as recalling its army of occupation and para-military forces. It should also direct its administration to execute the writ of 'Khalistan'.

'Khalistan', for the time being, does not intend to bring about any change in the present form of government/administration set up, so that day-to-day work may not suffer. Only the seals of Government of Punjab and India will be replaced by those of 'Khalistan'.

The Sikh community is especially commanded to be patient and tolerant. The Government Sikh officials, the Sikh soldiers and all kind of Government/semi-Government employees should, without falling victim to any provocation, continue to do their duty honestly, till some specific orders from the Panth. We are desirous of avoiding every kind of upheaval, especially the destruction of State property and (natural) resources.

The task of forming the Government of 'Khalistan' has been left to its Prime Minister/President who will announce its formation at the earliest. All Sikh political organisations are hereby directed to declare their concurrence and allegiance to 'Khalistan', and accord all possible help to make it a Success.

At this juncture, every Sikh is duty-bound to forge Panthak unity by brushing aside all kinds of differences.

Social Structure

'Khalistan' will function on the lines of the Guru's saying *"So long as the Khalsa remains distinguishable, I shall bestow full glory upon him"*[256]. No individual will be allowed to exploit others (either economically or socially), particularly the backward village community. Profiteering, black-marketing, adulteration, and all such other offences and social inequalities will not be tolerated by the Khalsa, which will also not allow mental retardation of any individual. No particular community or sect will be allowed to impose selfish will, arbitrarily upon others through the medium of press, writing, education or other media of publicity.

The constitutional arrangements will be made for the religion to act as the custodian of State. The Sikh religion will be the official creed of Khalistan. Further, it will be a paramount duty of the Government to see that Sikhism must flourish unhindered in Khalistan.

The Chief objective before the political and administrative structure of Khalistan will be the welfare of humanity and social service, as per the saying: *"It is sinful to employ our hands and legs, save in the service of others."*

Every Sikh, male and female, will be guaranteed to develop and prosper to the best of his or her ability. The lack of education or social backwardness will not be allowed to stand in the way of progress. The monopoly of education with its feudalistic tendencies, will also not be allowed to be used, as a tool to deprive the uneducated of their rights, just as the way in which the children of the urban settlers and the rich, outmanoeuvre all the children of the poor village folk and enjoy the bounties of nature much more than what is due. While on the other hand the children of the poor and the village people continue to

---

[256] This saying is from codes of conduct and is attributed to Guru Gobind Singh

remain backward, from generation to generation, due to illiteracy, poverty and sickness. The Khalistan government would like to base the distribution of all natural resources upon the fulfilment of basic necessities, of life.

Feudalism and capitalism will not be allowed to influence the government machinery and the consciousness of the people. Contrary to it, no limitation will be imposed on any individual to prosper and flourish according to the best of his wisdom, labour and ability.

The people will be associated fully with the administrative task and their participation will ensure that the red tapism will not re-emerge in Khalistan. At the village level, the local men will be associated with civil, criminal, development and judicial administration of various types so that the false witnesses and police touts may not kill justice by concealing the truth. The association and involvement of the villagers will be secured through more than one (it may be two or three) tier systems to see that opportunity for appeal and arguments may be readily available and at low cost.

The policy of Khalistan will be as per the Guru's wish, 'Sarbat Da Bhala' (welfare of all) and a policy of encouraging a civilized life, of promoting the sense of brotherhood of mankind and a sense of involvement. The segregation of humanity based upon caste, creed, birth, locality and colour will not be permitted, and such divisions will be abolished by the use of political power. Likewise, such other cruel and distasteful practices ascribed to social-inequality, especially between Sikh males and females will be removed through the use of political power.

It will be the first endeavour of 'Khalistan' to maintain cordial relations with its neighbouring countries.

The 'Khalistan Commando Force' is under the charge of General Hari Singh[257], its Commander-in-chief. This force shall serve as the nucleus of future defence, an organisation of 'Khalistan'.

The Sikhs living outside Punjab in India are hereby called upon to settle in Khalistan, so that they may not face any calamity such as the holocaust of November 1984. At the same time, money-minded Hindus are hereby directed not to put hurdles in the way of Khalsa Panth.

The Shahi Imam in Delhi, Saiyyed Muhammad Abdulla Bukhari, in his presidential address at the Sikh Seminar on "Why not Khalistan?' held at Chandigarh on February, 1981, while referring to the bloody massacre of Sikhs by Nirankaris on 13 April, 1978, at Arnritsar, had observed that in free India the Muslims had been subjected to carnage but now the Sikhs too are being butchered. This observation of the Shahi Imam has proved to be prophetic. The Indian Punjab Government has started the assassination of the Amritdhari (baptised) Sikhs in Punjab. The innocent Sikh youths, without being tried in the courts, are being killed in fake police encounters regularly.

The police chief of Rajasthan has complained about 400 such dead bodies found in the Rajasthan canal. Subsequent to this, in June 1984, the Government of India, under the cover of curfew, butchered the entire Sangat gathered at Darbar Sahib on the eve of Gurpurb celebration of Sri Guru Arjun Dev Ji. Following this, the armed forces besieged all the Gurdwaras of Punjab and killed the Sikhs

---

[257] This in actual fact Bhai Manbir Singh Chaheru (1959 – 1987) the name used here was his alias.

therein. Similar curfew was imposed on more than 12,000 villages of Punjab and Amritdhari (baptised) Sikhs were hunted down and martyred. Before starting this task of genocide of the baptised Sikhs, the Hindu military officers and sepoys were mentally and emotionally equipped through their official Magazine Bat Cheet for the complete extinction of the Sikhs. It was clearly spelt out in the Bat Cheet as to what were the distinctive marks of the Amritdhari Sikhs. It was mentioned that though outwardly they appear to be innocent, yet in reality they (Amritdhari Sikhs) are murderous, anti-national and extremists. Therefore, it becomes the duty of every security personnel to inform their superiors of the whereabouts of any such Amritdhari, Sikh they come across.

Nowhere in the history of the world, such an action has been taken by any Army against the citizens of its own country.

After this, when Indira (Gandhi) was assassinated by 'numerous bullets', the Hindu Government of India, the new Prime Minster, in league with his political and other official associates/advisers, executed the conspiracy of systematic killings of the Sikhs in Delhi for a number of days. This carnage has put to pale even the bloody carnage of Nadir Shah in Delhi.

Bhai Ajit Singh Bains, ex-judge, Punjab and Haryana High court, Chandigarh President of the Enquiry Committee constituted by the Barnala Government, while writing about the 100 false police encounters, expressed surprise over the fact that in none of these encounters, any police constable or an officer has been shown as wounded, nor any murder case has been registered against police. It is because in India, the government functions as per the saying, "O Lalo, falsehood is reigning all around[258]." This shows the real meaning of Brahminical principles which proclaim that only 'Truth wins' but practise falsehood. The singular aim of Brahminism is to exterminate the Sikh religion root and branch because the Sikh religion is inimical to the Brahminical[259] principles of caste-system and hypocritical actions.

It is what was done by Shankaracharya who secured the death of lakhs[260] of Buddhist monks and destroyed their temples and other religious symbols by the use of military forces. Although the Buddhist religion took its birth in Hindustan, and it spread in far-flung countries like China, Japan, Malaya and Burma etc, yet it was eliminated from its place of birth i.e. India. This reflects the real meaning of the Brahminical motto of Ahimsa Paramo Dharma (Non violence is the supreme religion).

Presently, the Indian Government is following the policy of Shankaracharya, determined to annihilate the Sikhs and Sikhism by using all kinds of political, cultural, economic, administrative and military means. This is the real meaning of the (false) claims of Brahminism, of preaching tolerance. In free India, attempts are made to put curbs on the minority communities/religions. The voices are raised in the Indian Parliament to put a ban on the conversion of the Hindus. A petition was made before West Bengal High Court to put a ban on the Holy Quran of the Muslims.

Attempts are made to secure a total annihilation of the Sikhs, destruction of the Sikh religious symbols through military force, imprisonment of the Kirtani Jathas

---

[258] Guru Nanak, 722, Raag Tilang, Sri Guru Granth Sahib
[259] This is in reference to the oppression of the high caste Brahmins
[260] A lakh equals 100,000

(singing groups), by registering false cases against them and threatening the Granthis (readers of the religious scriptures) in every village and involving them in false cases too, and putting then behind bars without trial. We have given details and already referred to the unequivocal anti-Sikh policies of the Indian Government and the manner in which the Amritdhari Sikhs, the products of the hard labour of Sikhism are being made the targets, for eliminationm through the methods as enunciated in the Bat Cheet.

The Government has already exhibited its anti-Sikh attitude by depriving the Sikhs of the fundamental rights through false propaganda of declaring the Sikhs as extremists, murderers and traitors. It has been quite successful in concealing the facts from the world through its use of political power. To achieve this aim, there is censorship and ban on the entry of foreign correspondents and newspaper editors in Punjab, since 1984. If any organisation or individual reported anything concerning the miserable plight and annihilation of the Sikhs, it/he incurred the wrath of the government which struck like a thunderbolt.

As a result of the false propaganda of the government, the Sikhs had to suffer several hardships even in the countries known as the champions of civil Rights such as U.S.A., England, West Germany and Canada. The Government of India, working by proxy (as a support of Brahminism), contemplates that the Sikhs shall depart from the scene like a Bulbul which submits silently to the will of her hunter. Unfortunately, for Brahmins, the Sikhs have been taught by their Gurus to walk on this earth proudly and gracefully like a lion. This is, in brief, the tale of undeclared total war of the Indian Government against the Sikhs.

The war had begun in June 1984 with the Operation 'Blue Star' and the Operation 'Wood Rose' (mopping up operation) continuing unabated till now. Some time back, when the Government of Bangla Desh banned the entry of Sikhs in that country and this issue was raised in the Indian Parliament, the Speaker Shri Balram Jakhar, most shamefully termed it as the internal matter of Bangla Desh. There is hardly any worse example in the world of such a big political communalism. All the major political parties of India i.e. B.J.P., C.P.L(M) organised themselves against the Sikhs and never condemned the massacre and the total annihilation of the Sikhs. This is the painful scene of the undeclared total war against the Sikhs. There is popular saying that history repeats itself. Today again, as per the writing of Shah Muhammad:

'Jang Hind-Punjab da hon laga, Chare Hindustani-Purbi-Dakkhani ji'.

(The war between India and Punjab has begun, and the Hindustanis belonging to the East and Deccan have attacked).

At this critical juncture we are (still) reluctant to declare a total war against India in retaliation (and have) only (retaliated) through declaration of Khalistan so that we may not be misunderstood and charged as aggressors in the world court.

If the Indian government does not stop the naked aggression, the five member Panthak Committee formed on 26th January, 1986, by the Sarbat Khalsa will approach the countries known for supporting the cause of human rights, for every kind of desired help, supply, assistance and sympathy. We appeal for similar help to the U.N.O. We shall, ever feel grateful to the neighbouring countries which sympathise with our cause during our hours of crisis. We are also grateful to those Sikh ladies and gentlemen living abroad, who have espoused our cause. If they so desire, we are ready to offer Khalistan citizenship to Sikhs living abroad.

The five member Panthak Committee appeals to all the Sikhs not to loot arms and ammunition or other items, from Sikh houses. It also appeals to the Sikh Sangats to help in every possible manner those Sikh ladies and gents who are engaged in fighting for the cause of the formation of Khalistan, since the (real) forte of the Sikhs, are the Sikh masses

Bhai Singh   Bhai Dhana   Bhai Gurbachan Singh   Bhai Aroor Singh

Bhai Wassan Singh   Bhai Gurdev Singh

Appendix 2
The Anandpur Sahib Resolution

As adopted by the working committee of the Shiromani Akali Dal at its meeting held at Sri Anandpur Sahib on October 16-17, 1973.

(A) Postulates

1. The Shiromani Akali Dal is the very embodiment of the hopes and aspirations of the Sikhs and as such is fully entitled to its representation. The basic postulates of this organization are human co-existence, human progress and ultimate unity of all human beings with the spiritual soul.

2. These postulates are based upon the three great principles of Sri Guru Nanak Dev Ji, namely meditation on God's Name, dignity of labour, and sharing the fruits of this labour. (Nam Japo, Kirat Karo, and Vand Chhako)

(B) Purposes

The Shiromani Akali Dal shall ever strive to achieve the following aims:

1. Propagation of Sikhism, its ethical values and code of conduct to combat atheism.

2. Preservation and keeping alive the concept of distinct and sovereign identity of the Panth and building up of appropriate condition in which the national sentiments and aspirations of the Sikh Panth will find full expression, satisfaction and growth.

3. Eradication of poverty and starvation through increased production and more equitable distribution of wealth and

the establishment of a just social order and any exploitation.

4. Vacation of discrimination on the basis of caste, creed or any other ground in keeping with basic principles of Sikhism.

5. Striving for the removal of disease and ill health, denouncement of the use of intoxicants and enlargement of full facilities for the physical well-being to prepare and enthuse the Sikh Nation for the national defense.

First Part

The Shiromani Akali Dal considers it its primary duty to inculcate among the Sikh, religious fervour and a pride in their rich religious heritage for which it proposes to pursue the following measures:

(a) Reiteration of the concept of unity (Oneness) of God, meditation on His Name, recitation of Gurbani, renewal of faith in the ten Sikh Gurus and the holy Sri Guru Granth Sahib and other appropriate measures for such a purpose.

(b) Grooming accomplished preachers, ragis, dhadis and poets in the Sikh Missionary College for a more effectively propagation of Sikhism, Sikh Philosophy, belief in Sikh code of conduct and Kirtan etc., at home and abroad, in schools and colleges, in villages and cities as indeed at every place.

(c) Baptizing the Sikhs (Amrit Parchar) on a vast scale, with particular emphasis on Schools and Colleges of which teachers and the taught shall be enthused through regular study circles.

(d) Reinculcate the religious practice of 'DASWAND' among the Sikhs. (Giving one tenth of one's earnings for the welfare of the Community).

(e) Generating feelings of respect for the Sikh intellectuals, writers, preachers, Granthis, etc., who also in turn, would be enthused to improve upon their accomplishments while conforming to the basic Sikh tenets and traditions.

(f) Streamlining the Gurdwaras administration by giving better training to their workers. Appropriate steps would also be taken to maintain Gurdwara buildings in proper condition. For such a purpose, the party representatives in the Shiromani Gurdwara Parbandhak Committee and local Committees would be directed from time to time to pull their weight.

(g) Making appropriate arrangements for the error free publication of Gurbani; promoting research work in the ancient and modem Sikh history as also its publication; rendering Gurbani in other languages and producing first rate literature on Sikhism.

(h) Taking appropriate steps for the enactment of an All India Gurdwara Act with a view to introduce improvements in the administration of the Gurdwaras throughout the country and to reintegrate the traditional preaching sects of Sikhism like Udasis and Nirmalas with the mainstream of Sikhism without in any way encroaching on the properties of their respective individual 'maths'.

(i) Taking such steps as may be necessary to bring the Sikh Gurdwaras all over the world under a single system of administration with a view to run them according to the basic Sikh norms and to pool their sources for dissemination of Sikhism on a wider and more impressive scale.

(j) Striving for free access to all those holy Sikh Shrines, including Nankana Sahib from which the Sikh Panth has been separated, for pilgrimage and proper upkeep.

Political Goal

The Political goal of the Panth, without doubt, is enshrined in the commandments of the Tenth Lord, in the pages of the Sikh history and in the very heart of Khalsa Panth, the ultimate objective of which is the pre-eminence of the Khalsa.

The fundamental policy of the Shiromani Akali Dal is to seek the realization of this birth right of the Khalsa through creation of congenial environment and a political set up.

For Attainment of this Aim

The Shiromani Akali Dal is determined to strive by all possible means to:

(a) Have all those Punjabi speaking areas, deliberately kept out of Punjab, such as Dalhousie in Gurdaspur District; Chandigarth; Pinjore-Kalka and Ambala Sardar etc., in Amabala District; the entire Una tehsil of Hoshiarpur District; the 'Desh' area of Nalagarh; Shahbad and Gulha blocks of Kamal District; Tohana Sub-Tehsil, Rattia block of Sirsa Tehsil of Hissar District and six tehsils of Ganganagar District in Rajasthan; merged with Punjab to constitute a single administrative unit where the interests of Sikhs and Sikhism are specifically protected.

(b) In this new Punjab and in other States, the Centre's interference would be restricted to Defence, Foreign relations, currency and general communication; all other departments would be in the jurisdiction of Punjab (and other states) which would be fully entitled to frame their own Laws on these subjects for administration. For the above departments of the Centre, Punjab and other States contribute in proportion to representation in the Parliament.

(c) The Sikhs and other religious minorities living out of Punjab should be adequately protected against any kind of discrimination).

2. The Shiromani Akali Dal would also endeavour to have the Indian Constitution recast on real federal principles, with equal representation at the Centre for all the States.

3. The Shiromani Akali Dal strongly denounces the foreign policy of India framed by the Congress party. It is worthless, hopeless, and highly detrimental to the interest of the country, the Nation and the mankind at large. Shiromani Akali Dal shall extend its support only to that foreign policy of India which is based on the principles of peace and national interests. It strongly advocates a policy of peace with all neighbouring countries especially those inhabited by the Sikhs and their sacred shrines. The Akali Dal is of the firm view that our foreign policy should in no case play second fiddle to that of any other country.

4. The Shiromani Akali Dal shall raise its firm voice against any discrimination against any Sikh (or even other) employees of the Central or State Governments. The Shiromani Akali Dal shall also endeavour to maintain the traditional position of the Sikhs in all the wings of the defence department and the Panth would pay particular attention to the needs of the Sikh army men. The

Shiromani Akali Dal would also see that 'Kirpan' is accepted as an internal part of the uniform of the Sikhs in army.

5. It shall be the primary duty of the Shiromani Akali Dal to help to rehabilitate the ex-servicemen of the Defence Department in civil life and for such a purpose it would extend them every help to enable them to organize themselves so that they are able to raise their voice in an effective way for gaining adequate concessions and proper safeguards for a life of self respect and dignity.

6. Thus, Shiromani Akali Dal is of the firm opinion that all those persons, males or females who have not been convicted to any criminal offence by a court of law should be at liberty to possess all types of small arms, like revolvers, guns, pistols, rifles, carbines etc., without any license, the only obligation being their registration.

7. The Shiromani Akali Dal seeks ban on the sale of liquor and other intoxicants and shall press for prohibition on the consumption of intoxicants and smoking in public places.

The Economic Policy and Programme of the Shiromani Akali Dal

As adopted by its Working Committee on 17th October, 1973 at its meeting held at Sri Anandpur Sahib:

Although the mainstay of the Indian economy is agriculture and all those political powers who claim to raise social structure on the basis of justice cannot afford to ignore this fact, yet this is a hard fact that the levers of economic powers, continue to be in the hands of big traders, capitalists and monopolists. Some marginal benefits might have accrued to other classes, but the real benefits of economic growth have been reaped by these categories during the last 26 years after independence. The political power has also been misappropriated by these classes which are wielding the same for their own benefits. As such, any peaceful attempt to usher in a new era of social justice would have to break the economic and political strongholds of these categories of people.

The Shiromani Akali Dal strongly advocates that the growing gulf between the rich and poor, in the urban and rural areas both should be abridged but, it is of the firm opinion that, for such a purpose, the first assault would have to be made on the classes who have assumed all the reins of economic power in their hands. In rural areas the Akali Dal is determined to help the weaker classes, like the scheduled castes, backward classes, landless tenants, ordinary labourers, poor and middle class farmers. For such a purpose, it stands for meaningful land reforms which envisage a ceiling of 30 standard acres and the distribution of excess land among the poor farmers.

T*he motto of Shiromani Akali Dal is to provide employment to all, requisite food and clothing for all, house to live in, suitable transport and to create means to fulfil all those necessities of a civilized life without which life appears incomplete.

As such, the economic policy of Shiromani Akali Dal shall endeavour to achieve the following objectives.

Agriculture Sector

During recent years the agriculture sector has witnessed land reforms and green revolution. The Shiromani Akali Dal undertakes to enrich the green revolution by an increase in yield per acre. It should also ensure perceptible improvement in the standard of living of all rural classes, more particularly of the poor and the middle class farmers, as also the landless labourer. For such a purpose, it plans to work on the following lines:

(a) Introducing land reforms and measures for increasing agricultural production with a view to remove the growing gap between the rich and the poor. For such a purpose the existing legislation on land ceiling would have to be revised and a firm ceiling of 30 standard acres per family would have to be enforced with proprietry rights to the actual tillers. The excess land would be distributed among the landless. Government land lying unused shall be distributed among the landless classes especially the scheduled castes and tribes. While distributing such lands, the interests of Harijans and landless labourers would be particularly taken care of. The Akali Dal would also consider other possibilities of allowing the tenants to service loans by mortgaging land under their plough, as also prohibiting the scheduled castes/tribes and backward classes from mortgaging the land distributed among them.

(b) The Shiromani Akali Dal shall work for the modernization of farming and would also try to enable the middle class and poor farmers to seek loans and inputs made available by different agencies.

(c) The Shiromani Akali Dal shall try to fix the prices of the agricultural produce on the basis of the returns of the middle class farmers. Such prices would be notified well before the sowing season and only the State Governments would be empowered to fix such prices.

(d) The Shiromani Akali Dal stands for complete nationalization of the trade in food grains and as such, shall endeavour to nationalize the wholesale trade in food grains through the establishment of state agencies.

(e) The Shiromani Akali Dal strongly opposes the demarcation of food zones and the attendant restrictions on the movements of food grains. The whole country should be treated as the Single Food Zone.

The party shall make special efforts to bring the Thein Dam and the Bhatinda Thermal Plant to a speedy completion so that increased and cheaper power and irrigation facilities are available. Efforts would be made for the establishment of an Atomic power station in the State.

Co-operative societies would be set up in the rural areas. In all those areas where canal water is not available small irrigation projects would be taken in hand.

Industrial Sector

The Shiromani Akali Dal strongly advocates that all key industries should be brought under the public sector.

It is of the opinion that basic consumer industries should be immediately nationalized to stabilise the prices of the consumer goods and to save the poor consumer from exploitation at the hands of the industrialists and the middlemen.

The pubic Sector industries should be established in such a way that the imbalance between different states is removed. A planned effort to establish agro-industries in the rural areas should be made to relieve the growing population pressure in the urban areas. The industrial management should be democratized by enabling the workers to have a say in the management and by fair distribution of profits between the industrialists and the workers. The credit agencies, especially the nationalized banks, should be directed to invest a fixed ratio of their deposits in the rural areas. Every industrial unit beyond worth one crore assets should be brought under the public sector. The Akali Dal stands for progressive nationalisation of transport.

The Public Sector units should be fully autonomous and manned by competent young executives-drawn from a central pool of talent.

Economic Policy

The Shiromani Akali Dal demands that the whole tax structure be revised in such a way that the evasion of taxes and the flow of black money is completely eradicated. It stands for a simple and straight-forward system of taxation. The present infra-structure of taxation, weighs heavily against the poor and enables the rich to bypass it. The party stands for a more realistic policy in this respect so that the black money running a parallel economy may be usefully utilized for workers, middle class employees and agricultural labour.

For their benefits the Shiromani Akali Dal would try its best:

1. To fix need based wages for industrial workers.
2. To bring progressive improvement in the standard of living of government employees.
3. To re-assess the minimum wages of agricultural labour and to standard of living for them.
4. To take necessary steps to provide roofed accommodation for standard of living for them.

5. To take necessary steps to provide roofed accommodation for the rural and urban poor.

Unemployment

The Shiromani Akali Dal Stands for full employment in the country. For such a purpose, it is of the firm opinion that the government must provide immediate employment to the educated and trained persons, otherwise reasonable unemployment allowance should be paid to them. This amount should be shared by the Centre and the State governments. The minimum rates (these rates were fixed in 1973) of such an allowance should be as under:

1. Matric and trained hands, Rs. 50/- per month
2. B.A., Rs. 75/- per month
3. M.A., Rs. 100/- per month
4. Engineers and Doctors, Rs. 150/- per month
5. Other trained Labour, Rs. 50/- per month

All persons above the age of 65 should be given old age pension.

Weaker Sections And Backward Classes

The Shiromani Akali Dal shall try to improve the economic condition of the backward classes and weaker sections of society by extending them facilities for education, employment and other concessions, to enable them to come at par with other sections of society. Food grains at cheaper rates would , be made available to them.

The Resolutions

Adopted, in the light of the Anandpur Sahib Resolution, at open session of the 18th All India Akali Conference held at

Ludhiana on October 28-29, 1978, under the presidentship of Jathedar Jagdev Singh Talwandi are as under:

Resolution No. 1

Moved by Sardar Gurcharan Singh Tohra, President, Shiromani Gurdwara Parbandhak Committee, and endorsed by Sardar Parkash Singh Badal, Chief Minister, Punjab.

The Shiromani Akali Dal realizes that India is a federal and republican geographical entity of different languages, religions and cultures. To safeguard the fundamental rights of the religious and linguistic minorities, to fulfil the demands of the democratic traditions and to pave the way for economic progress, it has become imperative that the Indian constitutional infrastructure should be given a real federal shape by redefining the Central and State relation and rights on the lines of the aforesaid principles and objectives.

The concept of total revolution given by Lok Naik Jaya Parkash Narain is also based upon the progressive decentralization of powers. The climax of the process of centralization of powers of the states through repeated amendments of the Constitution during the Congress regime came before the countrymen in the form of the Emergency (1975), when all fundamental rights of all citizens was usurped. It was then that the programme of decentralization of powers ever advocated by Shiromani Akali Dal was openly accepted and adopted by other political parties including Janata Party, C.P.I. (M), D.M.K., etc.

Shiromani Akali Dal has ever stood firm on this principle and that is why after a very careful consideration it unanimously adopted a resolution to this effect first at the

All India Akali Conference, Batala, then at Anandpur Sahib which has endorsed the principle of State autonomy in keeping with the concept of federalism.

As such, the Shiromani Akali Dal emphatically urges upon the Janata Government to take cognizance of the different linguistic and cultural sections, religious minorities as also the voice of millions of people and recast the constitutional structure of the country on real and meaningful federal principles to obviate the possibility of any danger to the unity and integrity of the country and, further, to enable the states to play a useful role for the progress and prosperity of the Indian people in their respective areas by a meaningful exercise of their powers.

Resolution No. 2

This momentous meeting of the Shiromani Akali Dal calls upon the Government of India to examine carefully the long tale of the excesses, wrongs, illegal actions committed by the previous Congress Government, more particularly during the Emergency, and try to find an early solution to the following problems:

   a. Chandigarh originally raised as a Capital for Punjab should be handed over to Punjab.
   b. The long-standing demand of the Shiromani Akali Dal for the merger in Punjab of the Punjabi-speaking areas, to be identified by linguistic experts with village as a unit, should be conceded.
   c. The control of headworks should continue to be vested in Punjab and, if need be, the Reorganization Act should be amended.
   d. The arbitrary and unjust Award given by Mrs. Indira Gandhi during the Emergency on the distributions of Ravi-Beas waters should be revised

on the universally accepted norms and principles, and justice be done to Punjab.
e. Keeping in view the special aptitude and martial qualities of the Sikhs, the present ratio of their strength in the Army should be maintained.
f. The excesses being committed on the settlers in the Tarai region of the Uttar Pradesh in the name of Land Reforms should be vacated by making suitable amendments in the ceiling law on the Central guidelines.

Resolution No. 3 (Economic Policy Resolution)

The chief sources of inspiration of the economic policies and programme of the Shiromani Akali Dal are the secular, democratic and socialistic concepts of Guru Nanak and Guru Gobind Singh. Our economic programme is based on three principles:

a. Dignity of labour
b. An economic and social structure which provides for the uplift of the poor and depressed sections of society.
c. Unabated opposition to concentration of economic and political power in the hands of the capitalists.

While drafting its economic policies and programme, the Shiromani Akali Dal in its historic Anandpur Sahib Resolution has laid particular stress on the need to break the monopolistic hold of the capitalists foisted on the Indian economy by 30 years of Congress rule in India. This capitalist hold enabled the Central government to assume all powers in its hands after the manner of Mughal imperialism. This was bound to thwart the economic progress of the states and injure the social and economic interests of the people. The Shiromani Akali Dal once again reiterates the Sikh way of life by resolving to fulfil the holy words of Guru Nanak Dev:

"He alone realizes the true path who labours honestly and shares with others the fruits of that labour".

This way of life is based upon three basic principles:

i. Doing honest labour.
ii. Sharing with others the fruits of this labour.
iii. Meditation on the Lord's Name.

The Shiromani Akali Dal calls upon the Central and the State governments to eradicate unemployment during the next ten years. While pursuing this aim, special emphasis should be laid on amelioration the lot of the weaker sections, scheduled and depressed classes, workers, landless and poor farmers and urban poor farmers and urban poor. Minimum wages should br fixed for all of them.

The Shiromani Akali Dal urges Punjab government to draw up such an economic plan for the state as would turn it into the leading state during the next ten years by raising per capita income to Rs. 3,000/- and by generating an economic growth rate of 7% per annum as against 4% at the national level.

The Shiromani Akali Dal gives first priority to the redrafting of the taxation structure in such a way that the burden of taxation is shifted from the poor to the richer classes and an equitable distribution of national income ensured.

The main plank of the economic programme of the Shiromani Akali Dal is to enable the economically weaker sections of the society to share the fruits of national income.

The Shiromani Akali Dal calls upon the Central government to make an international airport at Amritsar which should also enjoy the facilities of a dry port. Similarly, a Stock Exchange should be opened at Ludhiana to accelerate the process of industrialization and economic growth in the State. The Shiromani Akali Dal also desires that suitable amendments should be made in the Foreign Exchange rules for free exchange of foreign currencies and thereby removing the difficulties being faced by the Indian emigrants.

The Shiromani Akali Dal emphatically urges upon the Indian government to bring about parity between the prices of the agricultural produce and that of the industrial raw materials so that the discrimination against such states that lack these materials may be removed.

The Shiromani Akali Dal demands that the exploitation of the produces of cash crops like cotton, sugarcane, oil seeds, etc., at the hand of traders should be stopped forthwith and for this purpose arrangements be made for purchase by government of these crops at remunerable prices. Besides, effective steps should be taken by government for the purchase of cotton through the Cotton Corporation.

The Shiromani Akali Dal strongly feels that the most pressing national problem is the need to ameliorate the lot of millions of exploited persons belonging to the scheduled classes. For such a purpose the Shiromani Akali Dal calls upon the Central and State governments to earmark special funds. Besides, the state governments should allot sufficient funds in their respective budgets for giving free residential plots both in the urban and rural areas to the Scheduled Castes.

The Shiromani Akali Dal also calls for the rapid diversification of farming. The shortcomings in the Land Reforms Laws should be removed, rapid industrialization of the State ensured, credit facilities for the medium industries expanded and unemployment allowance given to those who are unemployed. For remunerative farming, perceptible reduction should be made in the prices of farm machinery like tractors, tubewells, as also of the inputs.

Resolution No. 4

This huge gathering of the Shiromani Akali Dal regrets the discrimination to which the Punjabi language is being subjected in adjoining States of Himachal, Haryana, Jammu and Kashmir, Delhi, etc. It is its firm demand that in accordance with the Nehru Language Formula, the neighbouring State of Punjab should give 'second language' status to Punjabi because of fairly large sections of their respective populations are Punjabi-speaking.

Resolution No. 5

The meeting regrets that against the 'claims' of the refugees who had migrated to Jammu and Kashmir as a result of the partition of the country, no compensation had been provided to them even after such a long time and these unfortunate refugees had been rotting in the camps ever since then.

This Akali Dal session, therefore, forcefully demands that their claims should be settled soon and immediate steps should be taken to rehabilitate them even if it involves an amendment to section 370.

Resolution No. 6

The 18th session of the All India Akali Conference take strong exception to the discrimination to which the minorities in other states are being subjected and the way in which their interests are being ignored.

As such, it demands that injustice against the Sikhs in other states should be vacated and proper representation should be given them in government service, local bodies and state legislatures, through nominations, if need be.

Resolution No. 7

The 18th session of the All India Akali Conference notes with satisfaction that mechanization of farming in the country has led to increase in the farm yield and a as a result the country is heading toward self-sufficiency.

However, the session feels that poor farmers are unable to tale to mechanization because of the enormity of the cost involved.

As such, the Shiromani Akali Dal urges upon the Government of India to abolish the excise duty on tractors, so that with the decrease in their prices, the smaller farmers may also be able to avail themselves of farm machinery and contribute to increase in agricultural produce of the country.

Resolution No. 8

This conference of the Shiromani Akali Dal appeals to the Central and State governments to pay particular attention to the poor and labouring classes and demands that besides making suitable amendments in the Minimum Wages Act, suitable legal steps be taken to improve the economic lot of the labouring class, to enable it to lead respectable life and play a useful role in the rapid industrialization of the country.

Resolution No. 9

This session seeks permission from the Government of India to install a broadcasting station at the Golden Temple, Amritsar, for the relay of 'Gurbani Kirtan' for the spiritual satisfaction of those Sikh who are living in foreign lands.

The session wishes to make it clear that the entire cost of the proposed broadcasting project would be borne by the Khalsa Panth and its over all control shall vest with the Indian Government. It is hoped that the Government would have no hesitation in conceding this demand after due consideration.

Resolution No. 10

The huge session of the Shiromani Akali Dal strongly urges upon the Government of India to make necessary amendments in the following enactment for the benefit of the agricultural classes who have toiled hard for the sake of larger national interests:

1. Hindu Succession Act be suitably amended to enable a woman to get rights of inheritance in the properties of her father-in-law instead of the father's.

2. The agricultural lands of the farmers should be completely exempted from the Wealth Tax and the Estate Tax.

Resolution No. 11

This vast gathering of the Shiromani Akali Dal strongly impresses upon the Government of India that keeping in vies that economic backwardness of the scheduled and non-scheduled castes, provisions proportionate to their population should be made in the budget for utilization for their welfare. A special ministry should be created at the Centre as a practical measure to render justice to them on the basis of reservations.

The session also calls upon the government that in keeping with the settlement already made, no discrimination should be made between the Sikh and Hindu Harijans in any part of the country.

Resolution No. 12

The Congress government is called upon to vacate the gross injustice, discrimination done to Punjab in the distribution of Ravi-Beas waters. The Central government must also give approval for the immediate establishment of six sugar and four textile mills in Punjab so that the State may be able to implement its agro-industrial policy.

Appendix 3

Akaal Takhat Edict 2nd June 1984 [261]

"Since long the Indian Government was planning to destroy the cultural identity of the Sikhs – Darbar Sahib, Sri Harimander Sahib. To execute this sinister plan, the C.R.P.F. has attacked the sacred shrine on June 1, 1984 with artillery fire. The unprovoked artillery attack in which a dozen Sikh pilgrims were killed and the sacred shrine of Golden Temple received bullet injuries, was the last murderous attack on the cultural and religious identity of the Sikhs. All the organizations of the Sikhs, present within the Golden Temple complex remained united and set a living example of steadfast confidence and rising spirit *(chardi kala)* of the Khalsa. Keeping in view the unprovoked attack on the Golden Temple, we appeal to all the organizations of the Khalsa Panth to defeat the sinister designs of the demoniac forces and repulse the attacks of the C.R.P.F. and B.S.F. to uphold the sanctity of Sri Darbar Sahib, Golden Temple."

Sd. Kirpal Singh	Sd. Sahib Singh
Jathedar,	*Head Granthi,*
Sri Akal Takhat Sahib,	Sri Harimandir Sahib,
SriAmritsar.	Sri Amritsar.
Dated, June 2, 1984.	

---

[261] Reproduced from, "Giani Kirpal Singh's Eye Witness Account of Operation Blue Star" (1999) 2-3, B. Chattar Singh Jiwan Singh, Amritsar

Appendix 4
Baatcheet – Indian Army Bulletin

June 1984

Serial Number 153

Introduction

1. It is amply evident now that the decision to employ the army in Punjab to deal with the tragic situation was taken by the authorities reluctantly as a last resort. Akali Dal could not be brought to the negotiation table. No final settlement could be accomplished. Unfortunately, the Akali Movement ultimately went out of the control of the moderate leaders and the extremists took over. The places of worship became their secure bases from where they carried out their unlawful activities.

THE ARMY ACTION

2. Being pledged to democracy and secularism, it has been a practice of the Government to honour the religious sentiments of every community. Accordingly, police entry into the places of worship was not permitted, although there is no written law which expressly prohibits it. Government showed utmost patience in dealing with the terrorists, who had taken shelter in the gurdwaras and were issuing death warrants, killing innocent people all over the country belonging to every community. Lawlessness prevailed over a long time. These terrorists, criminals, murderers smugglers and other undesirable elements wanted by the police, taking

shelter in gurdwaras, started organising themselves for anti – national activities. A large quantity of arms, ammunition and sophisticated transmitting equipment recovered by us during the action and Pakistani nationals dressed as Nihangs prove their evil design. Countries inimical to us and some disgruntled ex – servicemen also helped extremists by training them. The temples were converted into fortresses and unlawful activities continued unabated. Some of our innocent countrymen were administered oath in the name of religion to support extremists and actively participated in the act of terrorism. These people wear a miniature kirpan around their neck and are called 'Amritdharis.'

3. Under such circumstances, the Government had to act promptly and sternly, for the benefit of all of us, to protect the sanctity of our religious places and preserve unity and integrity of the county as a whole. Besides the police and the para – military forces, the military also had to be brought on to the scene to deal with the situation.

4. All have appreciated our Army's action. Our officers and men have shown unprecedented courage in facing the terrorists who indulged in the most brutal acts of even blowing up our men with lethal devices. The army has exhibited great restraint and discipline by not even pointing their weapons towards Sri Harmandir Sahib from where the terrorists continued to shower bullets upon them. Those whom took part in the action belonged to all communities. Having taken oath to maintain the sanctity of the holy place, they displayed indomitable will and unprecedented loyalty.

Everyone of us is proud of our men that even under great provocation they maintained their balance.

AN APPEAL

5. Although the majority of the terrorists have been dealt with and the bulk of the arms and ammunition recovered, yet a large number of them are still at large. They have to be subdued to achieve the final aim of restring peace in the country. Any knowledge of the 'Amritdharis' who are dangerous people and pledged to commit murder, arson and acts of terrorism should immediately be brought to the notice of the authorities. These people may appear harmless from the outside but they are basically committed to terrorism. In the interest of us all, their identity and whereabouts must always be disclosed.

6. We must always keep our eyes and ears open; never listen to rumours and malicious propaganda being planned and carried out by the enemy agents.

7. Our integrity and loyalty to the country could never be questioned. We have a long tradition of sacrifices for our sacred Mother Land. Our forefathers taught us to always live for the well being of the country as a whole. It is our bounden duty now to protect the National interest at all costs.

CONCLUSION

8. Army is absolutely an apolitical organization. Narrow consideration of caste, creed and communal feelings have never betrayed us. We belong to the country and re – dedicate ourselves to sacrifice for

its honour, unity and security. Whatever happened was unavoidable. We must learn a lesson from it that we do not fall prey to the designs of external forces.

General Sinha's Interview

The following is a transcription of relevant parts of this interview with General Sinha by Kanwar Sandhu. To view the whole interview, on can go to this link
http://www.youtube.com/watch?v=db5GX0LLN-4

06:24 (mins into interview)

Sandu:
Now, you've seen Kashmir from very close quarters in 1947,
then you Commanded a division in the 70s in Kashmir and later you were the Governor in the State of Jammu and Kashmir. Now as Western Army Commander you saw the Panjab problem from very close quarters and I remember in the early 80s you did not let the army get involved in the Mehta Chowk Gurdwara incident. What really happened?

Sinha:
"You see, there was a little history before the Mehta Chowk
Gurdwara incident. Defence Minister Venkatra ... had come
to Bhatinda and I as just an army commander, was there to accompany him on his tour, and during the tour I said "Sir I want to talk to you about the Panjab problem, the Akali problem" and he told me "General, that is a political problem. We don't want our Generals to get involved in politics"

So.."I suggest you're very right Sir, but apart from being Defence Minister, you're part of the committee of the cabinet negotiating with the Akaalis and I as the Western

Army Commander have certain views which I want to place before you, and of course it verges in politics, but at a certain level, there is a very thin line dividing strategy and politics. I have 3 reasons why I want to raise this issue with you.

Number 1, I'm responsible for the defence of Panjab (and he went to war with Pakistan) and if this problem continues to fester, it may affect my operational plans because I'll have to look over the shoulder. Because, what is happening inside, whilst fighting Pakistan forces, so I'll have to plan for that contingency.

The 2nd reason I have is that I am also responsible for internal security, if the police or civil state government cannot handle this situation, the army will be called in, so I have to be prepared for that contingency. And my 3rd reason is, that in my army of 300,000, there are 80,000 Sikh Soldiers, this problem may affect their discipline and morale."

So he then asked me, "What do you want me to do?" I said "All that I want you to do, is to resolve the problem. And how we do it.."

09:36
Sandhu: This must have been 1981?

Sinha:
A little before Mehta Chowk..."you resolve the problem, how you do it is beyond me"

He (Defence Minister) said "you know, it is politics." Then he turned around to me, "Suppose you were in my shoes, what would you do?"

So I said.. "Sir, as far as I can see, the Akalis have 3 demands. Number 1, Express Train, The Golden Temple Express. [Sinha Laughs] What is the problem? This should be done straight away. The 2nd demand, is that cigarette shops within 100 yards of the Golden Temple should be moved out. I said, that again, is so simple, shouldn't take us more than a couple of minutes, and shops which are being moved, give them a generous compensation. And the 3rd request is, that Gurbani be transmitted from the Golden Temple, I said why not? Not only the Sikhs, but I come from Bihar, people in Patna would welcome hearing Gurbani from the Golden Temple on the radio."

"So (the Defence Minister said).. It's all politics and you know in politics, you give an inch, you'll have to give a yard. Today, these are innocuous things, tomorrow the demand will come, declare Amritsar a 'Vatican City'"

"So I said, that demand has not yet come, and when it comes we can take a decision" ..and that ended. Then the Mehta Chowk episode took place.

11:39
Sandu: In Mehta Chowk i think you were asked to.. get Bhindranwale and his group out of the Gurdwara?

Sinha:
See, the situation was, that Bhindranwala was in Mehta Chowk. He had met Zail Singh the Home Minister in Delhi,
coming from Bombay with 30-40 rifles with him, no one

had done anything, and I was rung up by the Chief Secretary of Panjab, I think Puri was his name.

He said "General, erm.. Bhindranwala has to be arrested, he is in the Gurdwara and could you give us a few tanks.

So I said "look"

12:23
Sandhu: Give you a few tanks?

Sinha:
I said, it's a very strange request, the Army doesn't give weapons to the Police, it uses its weapons itself and when it is called in aid of the police, we use our weapons. We don't hand over our weapons like this, and tanks, Police were not trained to use it, so I don't know what you will do with it? And even if you have some ex-servicemen from Armoured-Core in the Police, they can use it.. the problem will arise, what are the repercussions.

"then" he (Puri) says "we wanted it, but if you can't do it, we'll have to do something"

After that I get a message from Darbara Singh, he was a Chief Minister, I went to see him.

He said "General Sahib, my Chief Secretary has told me that you cannot give us tanks and you have very valid reasons for it, and I agree with you. But do one thing for us, send the Army, arrest Bhindranwala and clear up the place."

So I said, "Sir, the Army has no powers of arrest, the Police can arrest, the Army cannot, and I would advise you to use the Police for that."

He said, "But Bhindranwala has got about 30-40 rifles."

So I said "So have you, the armed police, the CRP, use them" and then, he said in Panjabi "Tussi sanoo madatt ni kardeh" (You are not helping us)

"Well" I said, "I'm very sorry sir" and our meeting ended..

2 days later, my Chief of Staff General Puri, he got a message from Delhi. Orders of the Prime Minister. The Army has to go in and arrest Bhindranwala. And, as a good Staff Officer, he acted on it, thinking that I'll also do the same. And he passed orders down the line and the Gurkha batalions detailed to go to Mehta Chowk and I was informed at about 6 in the evening or 5.30 when I had landed. So, my immediate reaction was, stop that, cancel that order. And he said "But Sir, but those are the Prime Ministers orders", I said "Yes, so far as you're concerned, you have to carry out my orders. As regards with the Prime Ministers orders, I"ll deal with the problem myself."

So I rang up Venkatram.. and I said "Sir, these are the orders and I have told my people not to take any action tip I have my views presented to the Prime Minister"

15:46
Sandhu: So how did the Defense Minister react?

Sinha:
He was taken aback. He said "You're not going to carry out Prime Ministers orders"

I said "No sir, I will carry out the Prime Ministers orders, but my submission is, that I am an Army Commander, I should be able to present my views before the Prime Minister before she gives the decision, and after hearing my views she gives the decision you should go, I'll go"

He, the Defence Minister, rather reluctantly told me "Ok, I'll talk to the Prime Minister"

Couple of hours later I get a message, the Army can stand down, the task will be carried out by the State Government, I was happy.

16:35
Sandhu: So your efforts actually paid off?

Sinha:
Yeah, and in fact, you were the correspondent of Indian Express, and the next morning I saw the headline in the Indian Express that "The Army Commander Refuses To Send Troops to Mehta Chowk Gurdwara."

Well, I have not actually refused, but I have made a submission, were very close it, but it was not disobedience of orders, it was just presenting my views to the..

17:06
Sandhu:
General, I believe that after the Mehta Chowk Gurdwara incident, you laid down a procedure, that if the Army has to enter Religious Places, they have to follow a certain procedure. What was that laid down procedure?

Sinha:
I worked out that the situation would arise when the Army

would be called upon to go to the Golden Temple. The Police mis-handled the Mehta Chowk incident, gave Bhindranwala 24 hours. Bhindranwala came out, there was firing, and about 6 or 7 people were killed. Bhindranwala was taken to Firozpur Jail. And then, suddenly, 2 days later, he was released. Because they said, that he had been arrested for being involved in the assassination of Lala Jagat Narayan, the editor of Panjab Kesri. And then they discovered, after all this tamasha, that there's not enough evidence against him, so he was released, and he became a hero. And from there he went to the Golden Temple. And a very dear friend of mine, Subegh Singh, now he had joined Bhindranwala. Subegh had written to me only a month before that, from Golden Temple, a personal letter, saying that you resigning and leaving the Army is a personal loss to me. So, I said ke, look, all this is going to spell trouble for us..

18:42
Sandhu: You could foresee the trouble

Sinha:
Yes, a day will come when the Army will be called to go in. So I laid down a standard operating procedure

18:52
Sandhu: Is this laid down procedure in writing?

Sinha:
Yea, it was, but I don't know whether it's still there. But, what I had laid down, was that, when the Army is called out, we would do everything in a very transparent manner. We would invite some eminent Sikh gentlemen from Amritsar to come and witness what we are doing so that wrong reports do not come out. Secondly, I would request

TV Coverage of the whole operation, so that the people can see what we are doing. I would have a cordon round Golden Temple established so that no one can go out or come in, and announce to Bhindranwala and his people, we do not want to enter the temple, that is sacrilege for us as it is for you. You come out, give them time, 24 hours, 48 hours, or even more. And in the meanwhile, cut out electricity to them, water supply, to make things difficult and coerce them. Simultaneously I said, we should have a Sikh Officer commanding the operation, and the mixture of Sikh and non-Sikh troops. We should get a temporary Gurdwara established outside with a cordon, where we should offer prayers. Ke let the whole thing be resolved peacefully and the Army not forced to enter the Gurdwara. If in spite of all that he doesn't respond and we have to go in, then all troops taking part in the operations should offer prayers at our temporary Gurdwara before going in, have ensured that their heads are covered and take off their shoes, go barefoot. And when you enter, use minimum force and try and get the better of them. This sort of thing, filmed and presented to everyone, would have ensured that no sentiments of the Sikhs would have been hurt

21:26
Sandhu: General, looking back. do you think that if this procedure had been followed, the damage or the hurt that was caused due to Operation Blue Star could have been prevented?

Sinha:
Definitely, my honest feeling. Sundar Ji was given the order, do this by first light tomorrow morning, tonight, and his reaction was that I'll do it by day before yesterday [Sinha Laughs], and he went in. And when he found the going tough, he asked for sanction to use tanks, and the sanction was given, and they used tanks and you know

what happened.

22:01
Sandhu: But do you think it was a political blunder or was it a military botch up?

Sinha:
Both. You see, that Sundar Ji had become over ambitious. He was looking.. he was a brilliant officer, he was looking for a field marshals baton, and he was all out to please Indira Gandhi. He even ignored the, my Standard Operating Procedure which I had laid down for him, but when I was governor in Assam, I had come to Delhi and I was told that Sundar Ji was in the referral hospital for the Army. We went to the hospital, went to Sundar Ji's room and Sundar Ji couldn't talk and he couldn't write, he could only make gestures. He was looking very morose and he's trying to tell me something by doing this, I couldn't make out, anyway I came out. He was doing this to indicate beard and maybe he wanted to say something about Blue Star. Well I don't know what he wanted to say but a few hours later he died.

23:18
Sandhu: General why do you think the then congress government and the prime minister Indira Gandhi in particular supersede you?

Sinha:
You see, one of the reasons was my, me trying to put up my views on the Akali problem in Panjab. The other, was the fact that my father and JP had been very good friends, he, they'd studied together in college, I used to call JP uncle, he used to come to our house. So this JP connection was something which was like a red rag to Indira Gandhi. And the 3rd also, I've heard, that in the Army, I was a

crusader for re-organisation of our Higher Defence Command, Chief of Defence, of Staff Integration, of Service Headquarters, of Ministry and that the bureaucrats were not very comfortable with it.

24:20
Sandhu: Talking of the Chief of Defence staff, since CTS hasn't happened even today, does it disappoint?

Sinha:
Very much so. I'll tell you why, apart from what I'd done, I was Governor of Assam, and Arun Singh came to see me, and said General, you have worked on this Chief of Defence Staff problem, re-organisation, can you give me a paper? I said yes, I'll give you a draft paper, I thought I owed it to the Army. I wrote out a draft paper, gave it to him, he accepted in total, and the report that he submitted, recommending Chief of Defence of Staff and integration duly reflected it. It was approved by the group of ministers. I lobbied for it with both Bajpaye and Advani, telling them, but they found it difficult to take a decision, particularly when I'm told, this is of course CSA, that the bureaucrats approached Venkatraman, and Venkatraman had been President of India, he had been Defense Minister, and convinced him that CDS would not be a good thing, the Army will become too powerful, and Venkatraman went and met Bajpaye and said this, so they hesitated and said, we'll build a political consensus on this issue before implementing it…

Selected Bibiliography

1. Ahmed, Ishtaq **The Politics of Religion in South & South East Asia,** Taylor & Francis, 2011

2. Babbar, G. S. **Government Organised Carnage,** Babbar Publications,1998

3. Chopra, V. D. **Agony of Punjab,** South Asia Books, 1984

4. Dhillon, Kirpal. **Identity & Survival, Sikh Militancy in India 1978 – 1993,** Penguin Books India, 2006

5. Fernandes, Edna. **A journey into the Heart of Indian Fundamentalism.** Portobello Books, London, 2006

6. Gill, K.P.S. **Knights of Falsehood.** Har Anand Publications, New Delhi, 1997

7. Grewal, J.S, **The Sikhs of the Punjab**, Cambridge University Press, 1990

8. Guevera, Che. **Venceremos: The Speeches & Writings of Che Guevera.** Edited by John Grasso. Macmillan, New York, 1968

9. Hardgrave R.L. & Kochanek S.A. **Indian Government and Politics in a Developing Nation.** Engage Learning, 2008

10. Jaijee, Inderjeet Singh, **Politics of Genocide,** Ajanta Publications, Delhi, 1999

11. Kaur Amarjit, **The Punjab Story,** Roli Books, New Delhi 1984,

12. Kaur, Gunisha. **Lost in History, 1984 Reconstructed.** Sikh Spirit Foundation, 2009

13. Kaur, Harminder, **Blue Star Over Amritsar**, Corporate Vision, New Delhi, 2006

14. Kumar, Ram Narayan, **Terror in Punjab**, Shipra Publications, Delhi, 2008

15. Kumar, R. M. & Sieberer, G. **The Sikh Struggle: Origin, Evolution and Present Phase,** Chanakya Publishers, Delhi, 1991

16. Mahmood, Cynthia. **Fighting for Faith & Nation, Dialogues with Sikh Militants.** University of Pennsylvania Press, 1996

17. Mahmood, Cynthia. **A Sea of Orange, Writing on the Sikhs & India.** Xlibris, 2001

18. Malhotra, Inder, **Indira Gandhi: A Personal and Political Biography**, London/Toronto, Hodder and Stoughton, 1989

19. Marwah, Ved. **Uncivil Wars: Pathology of Terrorism in India,** South Asia Book, Delhi, 1996

20. Mazzini, Giuseppe **A Cosmopolitanism of Nations: Giuseppe Mazzini's Writings on Democracy, Nation Building, & International Relations.** Princeton University Press, Woodstock, 2009. Edited by Stefano Recchia & Nadia Urbinati

21. Mazzini, Giuseppe. **Neither Pacifism nor Terror: Considerations on the Paris Commune and the French National Assembly.** 1871

22. Mistry, Rohinton, **A fine Balance**, 2006

23. Mitta, Manoj & Phoolka, H.S. **When a tree shook Delhi.** Roli Books, New Delhi, 2007

24. Nayar K & Singh K, **Tragedy of Punjab,** Vision Books, New Delhi, 1984

25. Nehru, Jawaharlal, **Jawaharlal Nehru An Autobiography**, Oxford University Press, New Delhi, 1980

26. Pettigrew, Joyce. **The Sikhs of the Punjab**, Zed Books, London, 1995

27. Rao, A. et al, **Oppression in Punjab**, Hind Mazdoor Kisan Panchayat Publication by Citizens for Democracy, 1985

28. Ribeiro, Julio. **Bullet for Bullet. My life as a Police Officer.** Penguin Books India, 1999

29. Sandhu, Ranbir Singh. **Struggle for Justice**, Sikh Educational & Religious Foundation, 1999

30. Samiuddin, Abida. **The Punjab Crisis: Challenge & Response**, South Asia Books, 1985

31. Singh, Anurag (Translated & Edited), **Giani Kirapl**

Singh's Eye Witness Account of Operation Blue Star, B. Chattar Singh Jiwan Singh, Amritsar, 1999

32. Singh, Gurmit, **A History of Sikh Struggles Vol.2,** Atlantic Publishers and Distributors, New Delhi, 1991

33. Singh, Harjinder. **Game of Love.** Akaal Publishers, Walsall, 2008

34. Singh, Kapur. **Saachi Saakhi**, Navyug Publishers, Chandni Chowk, Delhi, 1979

35. Singh, Kushwant. **A History of the Sikhs Vol. 2** Oxford University Press, Delhi, 1991

36. Singh, Sangat. **The Sikhs in History**, New York, 1995

37. Singh, Zail. **Memories of Giani Zail Singh, The Seventh President of India.** New Delhi, 1997

38. Sinha et al, **Army Action in Punjab: Prelude and Aftermath**, Samta Era, Delhi, 1984

39. Sohal, Jay Singh, **Turbanology Guide to Sikh Identity**, Dot Hyphen, Birmingham, 2013

40. Tully, Mark & Jacob, Satish. **Amritsar, Mrs Gandhi's Last Battle,** Rupa, New Delhi, 1985

Selected Bibliography